CliffsNotes™
Writing a Great Resume

By Peter Weddle

IN THIS BOOK

- Gather the tools you need to write a powerful resume fast
- Tailor your resume to suit your career history and goals
- Use sample resumes to model the perfect resume for you
- Reinforce what you learn with CliffsNotes Review
- Find more great resume information in CliffsNotes Resource Center and online at www.cliffsnotes.com

IDG BOOKS WORLDWIDE

IDG Books Worldwide, Inc.
An International Data Group Company
Foster City, CA • Chicago, IL • Indianapolis, IN • New York, NY

About the Author

Peter D. Weddle is a businessman turned author and commentator. He writes weekly columns about employment for *The Wall Street Journal* and *National Business Employment Weekly.* In addition, he publishes "WEDDLE's, The Newsletter for Successful Online Recruiting" and WEDDLE's Guide to Employment Web-Sites.

Publisher's Acknowledgments
Editorial

Project Editor: Andrea Boucher
Associate Acquisitions Editor: Karen Hansen
Copy Editor: Linda S. Stark
Technical Editor(s): Perri Capell
Editorial Manager: Jennifer Ehrlich
Special Help: Kathleen Dobie

Production

Indexer: York Production Services, Inc.
Proofreader: York Production Services, Inc.
IDG Books Indianapolis Production Department

CliffsNotes™ Writing a Great Resume
Published by
IDG Books Worldwide, Inc.
An International Data Group Company
919 E. Hillsdale Blvd.
Suite 400
Foster City, CA 94404
www.idgbooks.com (IDG Books Worldwide Web site)
www.cliffsnotes.com (CliffsNotes Web site)

Library of Congress Catalog Card No.: 99-67163
ISBN: 0-7645-8546-0
Printed in the United States of America
10 9 8 7 6 5 4 3 2 1
1O/QZ/RS/ZZ/IN
Distributed in the United States by IDG Books Worldwide, Inc.
Distributed by CDG Books Canada Inc. for Canada; by Transworld Publishers Limited in the United Kingdom; by IDG Norge Books for Norway; by IDG Sweden Books for Sweden; by IDG Books Australia Publishing Corporation Pty. Ltd. for Australia and New Zealand; by TransQuest Publishers Pte Ltd. for Singapore, Malaysia, Thailand, Indonesia, and Hong Kong; by Gotop Information Inc. for Taiwan; by ICG Muse, Inc. for Japan; by Intersoft for South Africa; by Eyrolles for France; by International Thomson Publishing for Germany, Austria and Switzerland; by Distribuidora Cuspide for Argentina; by LR International for Brazil; by Galileo Libros for Chile; by Ediciones ZETA S.C.R. Ltda. for Peru; by WS Computer Publishing Corporation, Inc., for the Philippines; by Contemporanea de Ediciones for Venezuela; by Express Computer Distributors for the Caribbean and West Indies; by Micronesia Media Distributor, Inc. for Micronesia; by Chips Computadoras S.A. de C.V. for Mexico; by Editorial Norma de Panama S.A. for Panama; by American Bookshops for Finland.
For general information on IDG Books Worldwide's books in the U.S., please call our Consumer Customer Service department at **800-762-2974**. For reseller information, including discounts and premium sales, please call our Reseller Customer Service department at **800-434-3422**.
For information on where to purchase IDG Books Worldwide's books outside the U.S., please contact our International Sales department at 317-596-5530 or fax **317-596-5692**.
For consumer information on foreign language translations, please contact our Customer Service department at **1-800-434-3422**, fax 317-596-5692, or e-mail rights@idgbooks.com.
For information on licensing foreign or domestic rights, please phone +1-650-655-3109.
For sales inquiries and special prices for bulk quantities, please contact our Sales department at 650-655-3200 or write to the address above.
For information on using IDG Books Worldwide's books in the classroom or for ordering examination copies, please contact our Educational Sales department at **800-434-2086** or fax 317-596-5499.
For press review copies, author interviews, or other publicity information, please contact our Public Relations department at **650-655-3000** or fax **650-655-3299**.
For authorization to photocopy items for corporate, personal, or educational use, please contact Copyright Clearance Center, 222 Rosewood Drive, Danvers, MA 01923, or fax **978-750-4470**.

 is a registered trademark under exclusive license to IDG Books Worldwide, Inc. from International Data Group, Inc.

Table of Contents

INTRODUCTION

In today's workplace, having a well-written resume that's always ready is an important part of career planning. This book shows you how to develop a resume that highlights your qualifications for the job you want. It helps you select the best resume format for your employment situation and shows you how to organize your skills and experience to the greatest advantage.

Why Do You Need This Book?

Can you answer yes to any of these questions?

- Do you need to learn how to write a powerful resume fast?

- Do you not have time to read 500 pages on choosing the right information and format for your resume?

- Do you want to design your resume to work with the computerized resume management systems most employers use?

- Do you want to be able to send your resume over the Internet?

If so, then CliffsNotes *Writing a Great Resume* is for you!

How to Use This Book

You can read this book straight through or just look for the information you need. You can find information on a particular topic in a number of ways: You can search the index in the back of the book, locate your topic in the Table of Contents, or read the In This Chapter list in each chapter. To reinforce your learning, check out the Review and the

Resource Center at the back of this book. To find important information in the book, look for the following icons in the text:

This icon points out something worth keeping in mind.

This icon clues you in to helpful hints and good advice.

This icon alerts you to something to avoid or treat with caution.

Don't Miss Our Web Site

Keep up with the world of resume writing by visiting the CliffsNotes Web site at www.cliffsnotes.com. Here's what you'll find:

- Interactive tools that are fun and informative
- Links to interesting Web sites
- Additional resources to help you continue your learning

At www.cliffsnotes.com, you can even register for a new feature called CliffsNotes Daily, which offers you newsletters on a variety of topics, delivered right to your e-mail inbox each business day. If you haven't yet discovered the Internet and are wondering how to get online, pick up *Getting On the Internet,* new from CliffsNotes. You'll learn just what you need to make your online connection quickly and easily. See you at www.cliffsnotes.com!

CHAPTER 1
SETTING EXPECTATIONS

IN THIS CHAPTER

- Getting the most out of your resume
- Providing the information employers and recruiters need
- Exploring the different types of resumes

Your resume is one of your most important tools for finding and winning a great job. This one- to two-page document is both a record of your past and current accomplishments in the workplace and an advertisement for the capabilities you offer to other organizations in the future. In effect, your resume describes what you can do and how well you can do it for an employer who has likely never met you.

That information is critical to your success in today's job market. Employers are swamped with resumes from other job seekers, and only a well-written, high-impact resume can set you apart. It describes what makes you special by presenting a history of what you have achieved and a statement about the potential contribution you can make. A great resume convincingly presents your unique set of skills and experience on paper so that an employer invites you to an interview, where you can sell yourself in person. In short, a well-prepared resume gets you into the competition so that you have the chance to win your dream job.

Writing a resume can seem a bit intimidating, whether you're a first-time job seeker or a seasoned workplace veteran, a skilled technician or a senior executive. The process is, however, something anyone can accomplish, and everyone should. Yes, it will take a little time and effort; but no, you don't need a degree in English or a background in career counseling to prepare an effective resume. Creating a great resume simply requires careful preparation, attention to detail, selection of the right type of resume for your work background and objective, and thorough follow-through. Do these things, and you'll produce a resume that can open the door to exciting new work opportunities and position you for continuous career advancement.

Understanding What Your Resume Can Do for You

A great resume can help you accomplish two important objectives: It enables you to make a great first impression, and it presents your work credentials in such a way that you

■ Can compete successfully for great jobs right now

■ Are well positioned for career-enhancing positions in the future

Making a positive first impression

In today's fast-changing workplace, a great resume is one of the key components of success. It acts as your agent, a tireless advocate for your career interests and goals. If you're job hunting, your resume is the means by which you introduce yourself to employers and networking contacts. It is the document you use to establish your credentials when you apply for a position and to describe your background and goals when you prospect for job leads.

In most cases, your resume gives employers their first look at you. The document's content, clarity, and persuasiveness — all part of your care in presenting these recorded credentials — determines whether that first impression is positive and helpful or not. And making a positive first impression has never been more important in the job market. Research shows that employers typically spend just 15–45 seconds reviewing each resume they receive. That's all the time your resume has to convey your qualifications for an open position. The quality and impact of that initial impression determines whether you are considered for the position.

First impressions can also have a significant impact on your *networking* abilities. Connecting with others to uncover job leads is an important part of any successful job search campaign. In many cases, you're meeting people for the first time, and your resume helps shape their impression of you. A great resume that creates a positive initial impression can expand the range of people who are willing to meet with you and point you toward interesting employment opportunities.

Promoting your credentials

Even if you're not actively job hunting, a great resume can help you achieve career success. It's an effective tool for measuring your progress in acquiring new skills and experience.

Today, employment security largely depends on how deep and how current your occupational skills and knowledge are. Half of that expertise grows obsolete every 3–5 years, however, due to technological and other changes. As a consequence, you now must continuously replenish and improve your credentials to keep your career healthy and moving forward.

Despite its value, this requirement for lifelong learning sometimes slips in its position among your priorities. The demands of today's job can mask the importance of continuous self-improvement and preparation for the future. That's where your resume can help. It's a record of your personal development, both in the past and in the present. In other words, if you don't have to update your resume every six months or so — to document newly acquired skills or experience —

odds are good that your capabilities are falling behind — a fitting reminder that you need to invest some time and energy in their development.

Schedule a personal performance appraisal with yourself every six months. Use your resume to evaluate your progress in the previous six-month period and to set clear, achievable goals for the next six months.

A great resume can also help you promote your credentials to others. Traditionally, cultivating that kind of connection was something you did only in an active job search. In today's ever-changing workplace, however, marketing your credentials should be a continuous activity. It is the only way to protect yourself from unexpected disruptions in employment and to manage your career advancement proactively.

A well-written resume enhances both the reach and stature of your credentials. In the past, networking was limited to who you knew; today, it's based on who you know *and who knows you.* The key to advancing your career is increasing the number of people who are aware of what you can do and how well you can do it.

Your resume enables you to provide an accurate, up-to-date, and upbeat introduction to your track record on the job, and circulating it can help you extend your circle of contacts. That ever-expanding network of people who know about your capabilities in the workplace helps ensure that you are considered for as many opportunities as possible and thus have a range of options with which to work as you manage your career.

Meeting Employers' Needs

Recruiters use resumes to identify prospective candidates for their open positions and to screen candidates to select the best qualified for further consideration and interviewing.

Providing the information employers need

An employer's initial assessment of a resume usually involves one or more reviews to determine how closely the person described in the document matches the profile of an ideal candidate. In most cases, the information provided in the resume about a person's field of employment, experience, and skills is compared to the requirements specified in a position description or recruiting requisition developed by a human resource department and/or hiring manager.

Often, a quick evaluation is performed first to eliminate those individuals who clearly are not qualified for the position because they have no background in the requisite career field or lack adequate experience. Then a more detailed assessment is performed to identify those candidates who best match the position specifications and should be interviewed by phone and/or in person.

To best represent you in this evaluation process, your resume must present your qualifications in the right vocabulary and in the right place.

- ■ **The right vocabulary.** Recruiters look for terms that express the skills and knowledge required to qualify a candidate for the available job. Because most recruiters don't have a working background in the technical fields for which they recruit, the greater the similarity between the terms they use and the terms found in your resume, the easier it is for a match to be identified. So express your qualifications in the vocabulary of recruiters.

  To determine the exact words and phrases to use, check the employment ads in your local newspaper and other publications for positions similar to the one you're seeking. See how recruiters are describing your skills and background, and then include their terms in your resume.

- **The right place.** The sheer volume of resumes that employers must review for each position precludes them from spending more than a moment or two on each document. In such a situation, even qualified candidates can be overlooked if their skills and experience are hard to find in the body of their resumes. To make sure that your resume isn't missed for the position you want, summarize your credentials in a paragraph titled "Profile" and place it at the top of your resume, just above the experience section. Although other sections of your resume provide much more information about your capabilities, this up-front summary ensures that even a harried reviewer can quickly find and evaluate your potential match with an open position.

Understanding how employers process resumes

Today, resumes can follow one of two paths when employers receive and process them.

When you send your resume by mail or fax to an employer's human resources department, the document goes through several steps:

1. The employer quickly reviews the resume to assess its match with the requirements for a specific open position and/or the employer's general hiring needs. If no match is possible (for example, you're a pastry chef and the organization manufactures surfboards), you may not be notified, and your resume will be immediately discarded. If, on the other hand, your resume demonstrates the possibility of a match, you may or may not be notified, but your resume proceeds to the next step.

2. In most cases, your resume is then entered into a computerized *resume management system.* Employers now receive so many resumes from prospective candidates that

even small and mid-sized organizations have turned to these systems to help them organize and use candidate information. Basically, a resume management system enables an employer to store the contents of your resume in a database where it can be subsequently located for further review.

If your resume is not entered into a computer, it likely will be stored in a traditional paper-based filing system. In most cases, the original of your resume always remains in a file in the human resource department. When recruiters or hiring managers want to review the document, copies are made and distributed as necessary.

Because most organizations use copies rather than the original of your resume for internal distribution, produce your resume on high-grade white paper. Only your copy shop appreciates your using more expensive colored paper, and it's an investment that can affect the clarity of subsequent photocopies.

3. If you're applying for a specific position, your resume is next subjected to a detailed review to assess your qualifications for that opening. If you seem like a good match, you may be called by a recruiter who will conduct a telephone interview to obtain additional information and further evaluate your credentials.

4. The resumes of the best-qualified candidates are then sent either electronically through the resume management system or by paper to the hiring manager for review. Based on that evaluation, a decision is made about whether or not to invite you in for a face-to-face interview. If you receive an invitation, your resume probably will serve to help develop and organize the questions you will be asked. If you do not receive an invitation, your resume normally remains in the resume management or paper filing system so that it can be considered for future openings.

When you send your resume over the Internet to an employer or attach it to an online application form, the e-document goes through several steps:

1. Your resume travels cyberspace as e-mail. When it arrives, the employer downloads the message and quickly reviews your resume to assess its applicability to a specific opening or the organization's general hiring needs. If your credentials match a current or anticipated vacancy, the resume file is transferred to a resume management system. In many cases, the employer sends you a return e-mail message indicating the receipt of your resume and its status.

2. If you're applying for a specific position, the computer file of your resume is then retrieved from the system and subjected to a detailed review to assess your qualifications for that opening. As in the paper resume process, you may then be called by a recruiter who will conduct a telephone interview to obtain additional information and evaluate your credentials.

3. The resumes of the best-qualified candidates are sent electronically through the resume management system to the hiring manager for review. From that point, the process proceeds exactly as it does for a paper resume. A decision is made about whether to invite you in for a face-to-face interview. If you receive an invitation, the development and organization of questions you'll be asked will stem from your resume. If you do not receive an invitation, your resume normally remains in the resume management system so that it can be considered for future jobs.

Describing Different Types of Resumes

You can choose to create your resume in any of three styles and pick from two alternative formats for their presentation.

The three types of resumes are *chronological, functional,* and *hybrid.*(Chapter 3 helps you determine which type is best for you.) The two alternative formats are *electronic* and *Internet.*

The chronological resume

A chronological resume describes your work experience as history. It is structured around dates, employers, and titles, beginning with your most recent job and working backward to your first position in the workplace. This format enables you to demonstrate a steady progression of your work skills and responsibilities. On the other hand, this resume type also focuses the reader's attention on what you have done, rather than on what you can do. Indeed, the chronological resume is often described as the "obituary resume" because it's the perfect format for writing a worklife summary.

Chronological resumes are the most prevalent type of resume in circulation today — for many reasons. First, this account of a person's employment past is easier to write than either a functional or hybrid resume. It has a logical structure and requires information that the writer is likely to have readily at hand. Second, the chronological resume also makes the recruiter's job easier. It formats experience so that it can be quickly and accurately compared to the requirements for an open position and provides a reasonable structure for a follow-up interview.

The functional resume

A functional resume is a description of what you can do, arranged according to how well you can do it. Its organizing principle is your capabilities, not a chronology of your experience. In effect, a functional resume leads with your strength by focusing on your skills and abilities, regardless of when you applied them in your career. The details of your employment history are included only to the extent that they illustrate your functional expertise.

Functional resumes are not as popular as chronological resumes. They are more difficult to write and are not as easily used by recruiters. They require that you organize the presentation of your career information by the contribution you can make to a future employer rather than by what you did for an employer in the past. And they can be more difficult for recruiters to evaluate because they don't present your career in a traditional linear format. But functional resumes can be particularly effective in describing your qualifications if you don't have a long track record of work experience or if there are gaps in your work history — for child rearing, education, or to take time off — and therefore can't demonstrate an unbroken record of employment experience.

The hybrid resume

The hybrid resume, also called the "combination resume," attempts to combine the best elements of both the chronological and functional formats. It includes a brief history of your work record and a detailed description of your functional qualifications. Typically, you position the work history section after the presentation of your qualifications so that recruiters can quickly scan and evaluate your skills and experience.

Hybrid resumes are as difficult to write as functional resumes. Moreover, the addition of a work history section consumes space on your resume and can force you to cut information in order to keep the document at an acceptable length. Further, including two experience sections can cause overlap and redundancy in the information that you present. Nevertheless, this format provides almost everything a recruiter needs to evaluate your credentials: a summary of your past work record, plus a detailed description of the skills and abilities you can offer to a future employer.

The electronic resume

The electronic resume is a special format designed for the high-tech environment prevalent in human resource departments today. Many employers now rely on computer-based resume management systems to store and organize the resumes they receive from candidates. These systems require that your paper resume be converted into information that a computer can accept and use. The conversion is accomplished with a device called a *scanner*. Scanners are very sensitive, however, and can't process many of the standard features used in word-processed documents. Therefore, the only way you can ensure that your resume will be included in such systems is to reconfigure it to make the document "computer-friendly."

Electronic resumes involve adjustments to both the format and content of your resume. To help scanners "read" your resume, you have to eliminate all the underlining, italics, graphics, and other conventions you ordinarily use to structure and highlight your information. In addition, to help the computer find your resume in its database, you have to augment your resume's content with keywords that describe your background and skills. Finally, take precautions in producing your resume to avoid other problems that can affect its accurate processing into a resume management system.

The Internet resume

A growing number of employers are also using the Internet to acquire resumes from candidates. They post their open positions at their own Web sites and at commercial recruitment sites and even ask that responses to print advertisements be sent to a designated e-mail address. When you use the Internet to apply for these openings or to transmit your resume, you gain the advantage of speed. Your credentials arrive at the employer's human resource department where they can be processed and evaluated while the resumes of other job seekers are still working their way through the mail.

When you send your resume over the Internet, it usually travels in the body of an e-mail message. As with resume management systems, the software programs used to send e-mail don't transmit traditional printed documents well. The journey through cyberspace may garble their contents, rendering them unintelligible. To use the Internet effectively, you must configure your resume for online transmission. You have to convert it to plain unformatted text and narrow the margins of the document to a maximum of 65 characters. In addition, you must eliminate all Greek, mathematical, and business symbols from the body of your resume.

Don't send your resume as an attachment to an e-mail message. Many computer viruses are transmitted as attachments, so most human resource departments are now reluctant to open them.

CHAPTER 2

LEARNING THE BASICS

IN THIS CHAPTER

- Creating a resume with the right stuff
- Assembling the seven core elements of a great resume
- Debunking the myths about writing and using resumes

All great resumes embody features and principles that enable these communication tools to serve both your interests and those of recruiters. These documents clearly and emphatically communicate who you are — your personality, work habits, and style — as well as what you can do in the workplace and the great ways you can do it.

Recognizing the Hallmarks of a Great Resume

A great resume has four distinguishing features. Each of these features contributes to a positive first impression — in written form — and all of them are necessary if you want to make that impression linger.

A great resume sells your successes

A great resume promotes you as an employment candidate by highlighting your capabilities and accomplishments. It focuses on the successes you have enjoyed at work and the contributions you have made to other employers. Your resume is not the place to volunteer negative information; if asked, of course, you should provide a complete and accurate accounting of your employment record. A great resume describes the tasks you performed, the actions you took, and the benefits you delivered, all of which reaches beyond dull-sounding responsibility statements, such as "I was responsible for doing this or that." In short, a well-crafted presentation portrays you as a person who gets the job done, rather than someone who simply had a job description.

Some people are uncomfortable with proactively selling themselves. Pointing out your finest qualities is, however, the best way to differentiate yourself and your record. Selling your successes tells an employer that you understand what he or she is looking for and explains how, if hired, you are likely to perform on the job. Although you may feel like you're boasting, you're not. As the old saying notes, "It ain't braggin' if ya' done it."

A great resume tells the truth

A great resume is accurate and truthful. It portrays your employment record in the best possible light, but never by making misleading statements, fudging the facts, or exaggerating your role or accomplishments. Employers know that many resumes contain false information. As a result, they are now much more vigilant about checking employment dates, positions held, activities performed, and other details presented on resumes. And nothing will end your candidacy for that dream job more quickly than to be caught in a lie. So, don't risk it; rely on just the facts — without embellishment.

A great resume is error-free

A great resume has no spelling, grammatical, or typographical errors. It is neat, well written, and carefully edited. This type of resume gives employers two ways of looking at you: First, it provides the information they need to evaluate your employment record; and second, it affords them an insight into what you are like as a worker. An error-free resume demonstrates that you are a careful person who is attentive to detail and takes pride in your work.

A great resume is clear and complete, but also concise

A great resume provides everything an employer needs to evaluate your qualifications for a position opening. Being complete, however, doesn't mean overstepping "enough, already." A great resume is never more than two pages long. Leave out any irrelevant information and facts that do not substantially enhance your employment credentials. In addition, present your information in short, hard-hitting statements that are easy to read and understand. Avoid flowery or pretentious language, run-on sentences, and long-winded paragraphs.

Practicing the Principles of Writing a Great Resume

Every great resume has seven core elements, all of which must be present for it to be complete and effective:

- Contact information
- Objective
- Profile
- Experience
- Accomplishments
- Education
- Professional affiliations and awards

Contact information

Begin your resume by centering your name at the top of the first page. Use your complete name, but not any informal or nickname or such designations as Mr., Ms., or Mrs. In addition, do not give the document a title, such as "Resume" or "The Resume of _____."

Beneath your name, position your postal address, telephone number, and e-mail address, if you have one. This information is critically important because it enables employers and recruiters to contact you for additional details and, potentially, to schedule an interview.

Tip

If possible, provide a telephone number where you can be reached privately during the business day. Otherwise, use a private telephone number that will be answered by another adult, a voice mail service, or an answering machine. Then make sure that you check your messages regularly and return recruiters' calls promptly. Similarly, use a private e-mailbox — not one provided by your employer (which is subject to inspection) — to receive e-mail from recruiters. Check your incoming e-mail at least twice daily.

Objective

Your objective statement tells the employer what kind of position you're seeking and helps you organize your resume. Place this single sentence, which generally runs about 20–30 words, just below your contact information. (For guidelines on writing an effective statement of objective, see Chapter 3.)

Profile

A profile appears below your objective statement and summarizes your key skills, abilities, experience, and knowledge. It should be roughly the same length as an objective statement (20–30 words) and written in 3–5 bullets or short, descriptive phrases.

Remember

A profile functions as a billboard to highlight your strengths in the workplace, and by being positioned near the top of your resume, enables recruiters to assess your qualifications quickly and accurately. Your profile should be rich with keywords — the nouns and phrases recruiters use to describe qualifications similar to yours. Review the terms included in recruitment ads, job postings on the Internet, and position descriptions, if you have access to them. Then write your profile with recruiters' vocabulary, always ensuring that the information you include is accurate, clearly expressed, and persuasive. For example:

PROFILE

- 15 years of experience as a successful sales agent in the personal insurance industry

- Top performer in the Eastern Region for the past five years

- Experienced at both new account sales and current account management and growth

Experience

The experience section provides a detailed description of your work credentials. Because both the space on your resume and the time recruiters have to review it are limited, include information that clearly and directly supports your objective. Each detail should be designed to provide evidence of your skills and knowledge, your track record in applying these attributes on the job, and your potential to extend that capability into another organization and a new position. If you use a chronological or hybrid format, this section also details your previous employers, positions held, and locations. (See Chapter 1 for a description of chronological, functional, and hybrid resumes.)

In today's job market, employers are seeking very specific kinds of talent. They want to hire individuals who have demonstrated high levels of performance in their occupational fields and gained the kind of experience that prepares them to achieve similar success in the future. Therefore, your experience section should provide a focused, hard-hitting summary of what you can do, not who you hope to be. It is a place for fact, not dreams; achievable objectives, not wishful thinking.

Accomplishments

In most cases, your accomplishments are best presented as bullets in the experience section. These success stories provide two kinds of information to employers. First, they are the details that prove how capable you are in your occupational field. Because quantitative measures are often easiest to understand and have the greatest impact on the reader, describing your on-the-job achievements in numbers, rather than phrases, may attract the most employer attention. Here's an example:

- Increased sales by 30% in just two years

- Accomplished special project on time and within budget, producing a $150,000 profit for the company

- Managed a weather-related spike of 5,000 claims within 60 days by hiring and training five new employees

Your accomplishments also provide employers with information about your character. These glimpses into proven performance are a statement about the pride you take in your work. They describe your sense of commitment to making genuine contributions on the job. And they are a measure of the importance you attach to being the best you can be in your profession, craft, or trade.

Education

Your resume also presents your most important education and training credentials. Once again, what you say in your objective should determine what to include in this section. Cite past degree-track programs you pursued and any classes and programs in which you are currently involved. In fact, employers now look very favorably on candidates who recognize the importance of and take responsibility for keeping their skills current. Therefore, think of yourself as a work-in-progress; always be enrolled in a program that extends your skills and knowledge in the workplace and always include that information on your resume.

To describe your educational credentials, think about providing the following information:

■ The name of the degree(s) or certificate(s) you have earned or are in the process of earning

■ The specific field in which you majored or the subject you are currently studying

■ The institution where you did your coursework or are now doing it

■ The date your degree(s)/certificate(s) were awarded or the term "ongoing" if you have not yet completed the program

For example:

BS/Software Engineering Carnegie Mellon, Pittsburgh, PA 1971

JAVA Programming University of Connecticut, Storrs, CT Ongoing

Professional affiliations and awards

In the professional affiliations and awards section, cite the names of any professional societies or associations to which you belong, as well as any positions you have held, presentations you have delivered at annual or chapter meetings, and articles you have authored for publication. Don't include the citation you received for helping out at the local community center, but do highlight any activities or achievements that underscore your dedication to your field and demonstrate your improved competency. For example:

■ Member American Marketing Association — 1975–Present

■ Mid-Ohio Chapter President American Marketing Association — 1991–93

■ "Building Powerful Brands" paper presented at American Marketing Association 9th Annual Convention — 1998

Dispelling Resume Myths

Myths are plentiful on the subject of writing and using a resume. By avoiding the mistakes that misleading information can cause, you can create a more powerful resume and achieve more gratifying results with your credentials.

Ten common misperceptions about writing a great resume

Warning

To put together a resume that attracts the kind of attention you seek and expresses to an employer the qualifications that count, you need to consider the following stumbling blocks — any of which can trip you up as you travel along your career path.

■ **Resumes are easy to write and can be completed quickly.** This view has long been prevalent among those who ignore their resumes until they begin an active job search. The truth, however, is that writing an effective resume requires both time and effort. Anyone can do it, but it takes intensive self-assessment, careful preparation, and detailed execution, often with several revisions to get it right. The return on that investment is a resume that serves you well in the job market and helps you manage your career successfully.

■ **Once written, your resume need not be updated or tailored.** Your resume is actually a living document. You should constantly update and refine it to reflect your growth and development in the workplace. Continued refinement can help you gauge your career progress and ensure that your record is always ready and available for review, if an attractive opportunity becomes available.

■ **Page count doesn't matter.** Unfortunately, it does. Employers have limited time to review your resume and limited space in which to store it. Therefore, keep your resume to two pages, maximum, and use your objective statement to focus on the information that best positions you to compete for the kind of job you want.

To make sure that an employer correctly enters your resume into a computerized management system (see Chapter 1), print each page on a separate sheet of paper, rather than on both sides of a single sheet.

■ **The best resume identifies your previous responsibilities**. Employers are less interested in responsibilities than in work accomplished — what you did and how well you did it in previous jobs. Therefore, use action verbs to describe the tasks you performed, the actions you took, and the achievements you accomplished. For example, "Performed daily audits of all accounts payable activities. Corrected errors and updated records to ensure compliance with internal policy and external regulations. Trained new clerks and supervised their initial work."

■ **Your resume should state your salary expectations.** Your resume is not the place to make salary demands. Stating a salary requirement simply adds another issue that may cause an employer to reject you as a candidate. Therefore, focus your resume on presenting your credentials in such a clear and compelling way that an employer will make you a generous job offer that will keep pay talks to a minimum.

■ **Your resume should include references and personal information.** A recruiter expects you to be able to provide references when asked, so there's no reason to state "References available on request" or to note your references' names and contact information on your resume. Also, don't include personal information such as your gender, age, ethnic background, marital status, religion, height, and weight (unless such information is relevant to performing the job you're seeking).

■ **Your resume should state why you left your previous position or are leaving your current one.** This issue is likely to come up during your evaluation by an employer, but it is best addressed in an interview, rather than on your resume. Moreover, when providing such information, always avoid making critical statements of other employers and individuals. Negative remarks can cause recruiters to worry about what you would say if you leave their organization in the future.

■ **Your resume should include a recent photograph.** Employers must avoid any discrimination based on a person's ethnicity, gender, age, or religion. A photograph can lead to such a situation, so most employers don't want to see one included with a resume.

- **Your resume should include lots of graphics and artwork to make it eye-appealing.** Making your resume attractive is important, but complex graphics and even overly elaborate typefaces (such as Old English) take up space and make it difficult for your resume to be processed by computer-based resume management systems. The best way to highlight the information in your resume is to provide plenty of white space on the document. Using bullets and short paragraphs of no more than 4–5 lines breaks up your text and sets off important details.

- **You can write a great resume by simply filling in the blanks.** Avoid using "plug and chug" templates when writing your resume. These canned programs are available in software, on CD ROM, and in print workbooks. Their generic language and cookie-cutter look and feel are easily recognized by recruiters and undercut the impact of your resume.

Three common misperceptions about using a resume

Although not as common as the myths about resume writing, there are a number of misconceptions about how to use a resume effectively in a job search.

- **You don't need a resume to get a job.** Although every rule has its exceptions, a resume is normally your ticket into the job market. Recruiters are under intense pressure to locate and interview candidates and fill open positions quickly. If you don't have a resume, you slow down the evaluation process and increase the recruiter's risk of making a hiring mistake. Moreover, not having such an important document can create the perception that you don't take adequate responsibility for your career, which may raise a red flag about your suitability for the job.

■ **Your resume will get you a job.** Only *you* can get you a job. A great resume should intrigue employers so much that they want to meet with you. In other words, your resume can open an employer's door — giving you the opportunity to sell yourself — but after that, it's up to you. A resume is an integral part of a larger process that involves research, follow-up, and additional communications, all of which you must plan and execute effectively to achieve your job-search objective.

■ **How you send your resume to a recruiter doesn't matter.** The way you send your resume to an employer has an impact on its effectiveness when a recruiter is reviewing the document. For example, don't mail your resume folded into a typical #10 business envelope. Instead, send the unfolded pages in a 9-x-12-inch envelope so that they can be properly processed by the computer-based resume management systems now being used in most employers' human resources departments. Similarly, a resume sent over the Internet should be formatted and adjusted to ensure its accurate transmission via e-mail. (For additional information on resume distribution, see Chapters 8 and 9.)

CHAPTER 3

CREATING A GREAT RESUME

IN THIS CHAPTER

- Uncovering your employment objective
- Creating a statement that expresses your objective
- Selecting the right type of resume for your objective

The key to creating a great resume is to understand what you want the document to achieve for you and to select the best type of resume for accomplishing that goal.

Taking the First Step

The first step in writing an effective resume is to determine your employment objective: the specific goal you would like to achieve in your next job.

Setting your sights

Great resumes have a clear and distinct theme. Every detail included in the resume supports that theme and reinforces its impact on the reader. This theme is your *objective;* it has two elements:

- The attributes and circumstances you want in your next job
- A clear and positive relationship to your career and its advancement

In other words, your objective has both a near-term and a mid-to-longer-term purpose. The message you're conveying focuses on your immediate goal in the job market — to make very clear the kind of job, work, and employer you're seeking. Your objective also connects your past, current, and future jobs into an integrated strategy and direction for your career.

Determining your objective requires that you know what professional interests you have and what potential positions may allow you to express those interests. In addition, you need a realistic sense of your current skill level and expertise in your chosen field. You then can figure the level and scope of position for which you are competitive. Achieving such understanding involves both introspection and research. You must know yourself and the workplace and continually update that knowledge as you grow and develop and the workplace changes.

Taking stock of your interests and making sure that they are aligned with your work is necessary whether you're a first-time job seeker, a seasoned worker at mid-career, or a highly paid expert in your field. To help you with the process of self-exploration, use one or both of the following exercises.

The lottery. Imagine that you won a huge jackpot in the lottery. Suddenly, finances are no longer an issue. The mortgage is paid, money is put away for the kids' educations, and your retirement program is generously funded. Now, you can do whatever you want to do with your life's work. What would that be? What activity would get you up in the morning and give you the most satisfaction at the end of the day? Describe it in a few lines — either on paper or in an electronic document that you can refer to.

Your tombstone. You spend much of your life at work. Aside from your family, faith, and friends, your career is probably the most important aspect of your life. If you suddenly learned that you were terminally ill, how would you like to be remembered? What would you be most proud of having accomplished at work? What would give you the greatest satisfaction? Write your thoughts down.

If you're a first-time job seeker, you may have to research which occupations and specific jobs provide the opportunity to express these interests and abilities. If you are a seasoned workplace veteran who is in transition or seeking greater satisfaction in your work, you may need to explore alternative career fields. Whatever your situation, you can find such information at college and university career centers, state employment security offices, public libraries, and on the Internet. For example, America's Job Bank (www.ajb.dni.us) offers a Career InfoNet that can help you identify career paths and opportunities.

Getting help

If you need help pinpointing your career interests, you can find several assessment exercises available through professional career counselors and centers. These include the following:

- The Myers-Briggs Type Indicator

- The Keirsey Temperament Test

- The Self-Directed Search (SDS)

- The Unisex Edition of the ACT Interest Inventory (UNIACT)

- The Vocational Interest Inventory (VII)

- The Career Occupational Preference System Interest Inventory (COPS)

Expressing Your Objective in a Statement

Creating a statement that serves as your employment objective not only helps focus your resume but also keeps your career on track by providing a clear direction toward an outcome that represents success for you. In addition, you can rephrase your objective so that it tailors your goals and capabilities to the needs of specific employers and thus makes you a more attractive employment candidate.

Organizing your objective statement

Your objective statement should express two important considerations:

- Your desired outcome — the specific kind of work you want to do

- The context in which you want to do it — the title or description of a specific position

The statement should also indicate the kind of organization in which you want to be employed and the benefit you expect to achieve from that experience. The more specific you are, the better. Vague objective statements often lead to unfocused resumes that do not present a clear, hard-hitting message about your capabilities and interests.

Organize the information in your objective statement as follows:

Title or description of your desired job + the kind of organization for which you want to work + the benefit you expect to derive from your effort. For example:

OBJECTIVE

A store manager position for a leader in the men's retail cloth-ing industry where I can enhance my team-building skills and gain hands-on experience in profit center management.

Writing your objective statement

Use the following four-step process to write your objective statement:

1. Identify or confirm the kind of position that can best enable you to express and develop your skills and abili-ties. Describe the position or note its title in a few words.

2. Identify the context or organizational setting in which you most enjoy working. Do you prefer a high-risk/high-reward start-up organization, an established industry leader, an entrepreneurial culture, or some other kind of organization? Describe the context you seek in a phrase.

3. Determine what experience and skills you would like to acquire in your next job. Identify capabilities that will enhance your satisfaction at work and advance your career. Make a list of those benefits.

4. Integrate the results of Steps 1–3 into a clear and con-cise objective statement. Write that statement.

Placing your objective statement

When you send your resume to a prospective employer, make sure that your objective statement appears in the body of your resume or in the cover letter that accompanies your resume.

Traditionally, an objective statement shows up in the promi-nent position just below your contact information. This loca-tion helps to focus both the development and the interpretation of your employment record. In other words, your objective is the first section of your resume that you write and the first section that an employer normally reads. This focal point acts as a lens through which

■ You evaluate the various details of your work record to determine what to include and what to discard

■ Employers assess your potential fit with their organization and position opening

By including only information that explains and supports your objective statement in your resume, you create a document with a focused and forceful message that helps employers make accurate judgments of your interests and abilities.

Space on a resume is limited, however, which means that you may have to remove your objective statement from the document. This section is the only part of your resume where you have an option to save space, and such a move is feasible only because you've used your objective as the basis for developing all the other information you've included. Indeed, only remove the statement *after* you complete the final draft of your resume to ensure that every detail included in the document is relevant and appropriate.

If you decide to omit your objective statement from your resume, you can still communicate this important message to prospective employers. Your cover letter, which should be a companion to every resume you send out to an employer, is an appropriate place to share a statement of your employment objective. This letter should relate your background, as described on your resume, to the requirements of the job or that specific employer's needs. To reinforce your qualifications, include your objective as a key point in your cover letter.

Translating your objective statement for employers

Your objective in the workplace is different from that of an employer. For example, your objective may be to obtain a position that would support your ambitions to be the most respected sales representative in your industry. An employer, however, seeks to fill that position with a sales representative who delivers consistent revenue and profit growth. Similarly, your objective might be to acquire a position with a higher salary, while the employer wants to recruit a candidate who can get the job done on time and within budget.

As a consequence, your objective statement must play two very different roles:

■ As a statement of what's important to you in the workplace, your objective's purpose is to focus the development of your resume. The act of creating an objective statement can help you home in on what's relevant and what's immaterial to the presentation of your credentials, which can tell you what to include — and exclude.

■ As a statement of what's important to an employer, your objective's role is to help sell your qualifications for a specific open position. A well-defined statement can differentiate you from other candidates by underscoring the close fit between your workplace goal and your employer's interests.

To play the second role, you have to translate your objective statement from its original expression of your hopes and ambitions to one that addresses the needs of an employer. Whether the statement appears in your resume or in a cover letter, this shift in focus is key to making a connection with a prospective employer's own objectives. In addition, you should tailor this revision to each employer's specific circumstances. Use the following steps to accomplish the translation:

1. Identify the title of the position you seek in an employer's organization. If available, use the exact title provided in the organization's advertisement or job announcement.

2. Pinpoint the benefits you can provide an organization with your skills and experience. To determine which benefits are of most interest to a specific employer, review the information contained in its recruitment ad or job posting. Look for descriptive terms that indicate a desired quality or outcome, such as "Looking for a fast-starter" or "Seek a manager who can control costs and build revenues." Decide which of the benefits you are most capable of providing.

3. Identify the organization where the open position is located. Be as specific as possible. For example, if you are applying for a position in the Engineering Division of Xerox Corporation, include the division name as well as that of the corporation.

4. Combine the results of Steps 1–3 into a clear and concise objective statement that expresses your goal in terms relevant to an employer. Write out your objective statement. For example:

OBJECTIVE

A sales representative position in the Xerox Engineering Division where I can apply my skills and 10 years of experience to generate improved revenues at lower costs.

Rewriting your objective statement for a specific employer has real impact, whether it appears in your resume or in a cover letter. The effort shows an employer that you

■ Have done your homework and identified the employer's needs

- Are serious enough about your application to tailor your objective to a specific employer

- Understand how to apply your skills and experience to meet the employer's needs.

Pinpointing the Right Type of Resume for You

When it comes to expressing your credentials, you can choose from several different types of formats to fit the needs of your resume and its intended audience. The three most commonly used styles have their strengths and limitations, and no single setup can effectively serve the unique circumstances and interests of every person. Therefore, an important key to developing a great resume is the selection of the best type for your particular circumstances.

Understanding the differences

Table 3-1 summarizes the differences between the three main types of resumes.

Table 3-1:   Characteristics of Different Resume Types

Name	Characteristics
Chronological	Organizes employment information in a historical format, beginning with your most recent job.
	Identifies each position you held by its title, the employer's name and location, and the dates you held it.
	Provides a brief description of what you did and your accomplishments in each position.

(continued)

Table 3-1: Characteristics of Different Resume Types (continued)

Name	Characteristics
Functional	Organizes employment information according to your skills and abilities, beginning with your strongest competency.
	Describes your level of expertise in each skill by presenting illustrative situations in which you applied the skill successfully on the job.
Hybrid	Includes both a brief chronological summary of your work experience and a description of your functional expertise.
	The chronological summary lists the title of each position you held, the employer's name and location, and the dates you worked there.
	The functional description illustrates your level of expertise in selected skills and abilities by presenting situations in which you applied them on the job.

In most cases, these differences are most evident in the experience section of your resume. They have little or no impact on the placement and content of your objective, profile, education, or professional affiliations and awards.

Within the experience section, the differences clearly affect the kind of information that you include in the resume, how you present that information, and the priority you give it. Those factors, in turn, give each resume format unique strengths and limitations with regard to its ability to represent a person's credentials effectively. These strengths and limitations are summarized in Table 3-2.

Table 3-2:   Strengths and Limitations of Different Resume Types

Chronological: Strengths	*Limitations*
Easy to read and understand	Inadequate space to describe skills fully
Emphasizes steady, continuous progression	Spotlights breaks in employment
Recognized and accepted by employers and recruiters	Doesn't describe nontraditional career paths well
Functional: Strengths	*Limitations*
Highlights what you can do and how well you can do it	Lack of an employment history makes it difficult for recruiters to evaluate you
Enables you to present your qualifications according to your level of expertise	Is difficult to write because you must synthesize your record into skill areas
Effectively describes experience gained via nontraditional career paths	Doesn't describe organizational advancement
Hybrid: Strengths	*Limitations*
Combines most strengths of both other types of resumes	Not enough space to detail your work record or qualifications completely
Clear presentation of your employment history	Unusual format may be uncomfortable for some employers and recruiters
Highlights what you can do and how well you can do it	

Selecting the best resume type for you

The characteristics of each resume type and its resulting strengths and limitations make it a more appropriate choice for some individuals than for others. The determining factors are your career path up to the present time and your skill profile. To select the best resume type for you and to learn how to write it, see Table 3-3. The following definitions can help you interpret the information in Table 3-3:

■ Your career path is said to be *uninterrupted* if you have had no breaks in employment of more than 30 days. An interrupted career path can be caused by such situations as unemployment, a period at home to raise children, an illness, or time spent pursuing an educational degree.

■ Your skill profile is *technical* if your objective involves the continuous development of your expertise in a particular field of knowledge or profession. Otherwise, your skill profile is *general* or *managerial.*

This table covers everyone in the workforce except first-time job seekers who lack a lengthy work record. If you are looking for your first full-time job, the functional resume is the best format for you. However, you should modify this format to reflect your special strengths. See Chapter 7 for more information on resumes for first-time employment.

Table 3-3: Selecting the Appropriate Resume Type for You

Career Path to Date	Skill Profile	Resume Type	Chapter in This Book
Uninterrupted	Technical	Hybrid	6
Uninterrupted	General or Managerial	Chronological	4
Interrupted	Technical	Functional	5
Interrupted	General or Managerial	Functional	5

CHAPTER 4

WRITING A CHRONOLOGICAL RESUME

IN THIS CHAPTER

- Making sure that a chronological resume is best for you
- Getting the content right
- Getting the format right

A chronological resume presents a history of your employment record, beginning with your most recent position. It identifies the title of each position you held, the organization which employed you, the dates you held the positions, and the tasks you performed.

Knowing When to Use a Chronological Resume

A chronological resume has several important strengths that make this format a good choice for some job seekers, as well as certain limitations that can degrade its effectiveness for other applicants.

Examining the strengths

As noted in Chapter 3, a chronological resume is usually best if you have a general or managerial background. This kind of resume is:

- **Easy to read and understand.** Recruiters can quickly determine what you have done in your career, the industries in which you have experience, and the kinds of organizations for which you've worked.

- **A record of continuous progression.** A chronological resume effectively chronicles steady development by presenting your work experience as an unbroken succession of positions with ever-increasing responsibility.

- **Recognized and accepted by employers and recruiters.** The chronological resume is the most prevalent type in the workplace, so recruiters and employers are familiar with the format and comfortable using the information it provides to evaluate candidates.

Exploring the weaknesses

For some job seekers, the chronological resume may not be the best choice of formats for presenting a package of qualifications. Relying on a historical perspective

- **Often doesn't fully describe your functional capabilities.** Depending on the length of your experience in the workplace, your complete employment history can consume much of the space on a two-page resume and prevent you from presenting all your skills and abilities.

- **Emphasizes breaks in employment.** By providing a historical record of your employment, a chronological resume makes it easy for recruiters to identify interruptions in your career or frequent job changes.

- **Doesn't effectively describe nontraditional career paths.** Because it's designed to describe your career as a succession of employers and positions with ever-increasing responsibility, a chronological resume is not able to portray alternative career paths — whether they involve periods of unemployment devoted to travel or some other interest or a series of different and unrelated occupational experiences — to the best advantage.

Based on these factors, a chronological resume can best serve you if your career has involved a steady, continuous series of positions in which you performed increasingly more challenging and important work. This style probably will not serve you well if you're a first-time job seeker with little or no work experience or if your career has followed a nontraditional path.

To develop your chronological resume, use the following seven-step process:

1. Collect your employment information. Include any position descriptions and recruitment ads for your previous or current jobs, performance appraisals, project or work descriptions, awards and other professional recognition (such as a certificate of achievement for project contributions), educational record and certificates of completion for training programs, and materials describing your affiliation and participation with professional organizations.

2. Organize your materials into chronological order, beginning with your most recent position and working back to your first job.

3. Prioritize the materials. Use your objective statement (refer to Chapter 3) to determine three categories of information:

Critical to supporting your objective and must be included

Helpful in supporting your objective and should be included if space permits

Not essential in supporting your objective and can be omitted

4. Write a first draft of your resume. See the detailed instructions for developing the content and format of your chronological resume in the next section of this chapter.

5. Revise your draft. Modify the information you've presented and, if necessary, delete selected segments in order to achieve a maximum length of two pages. Only delete information you consider helpful but not critical to supporting your objective.

6. Edit your draft. Carefully review your draft for misspellings and grammatical, typographical, and other errors. Then ask a friend to review the document to catch any errors you may have missed and to check that the information is easy to read and understand.

7. Produce your resume. Use a laser printer to print your resume, or have the document reproduced at a professional print shop. Use a font size of 11–12 points, high-quality white paper, and black ink. Print each page on a separate sheet of paper rather than on the front and back of the same page.

Developing the Content of Your Chronological Resume

Use the following checklist to develop a great chronological resume. Build your contact information and profile, education, and professional affiliations and awards sections first, and then develop the all-important experience section. If you need additional information, refer to Chapter 2.

Contact information

1. Center your full name at the top of the page. Include your middle initial, if appropriate, but not your middle name, unless you use it at work.

2. After your name, add the appropriate acronym for any certifications you have received from recognized independent certifying organizations (for example, CPA for Certified Public Accountant).

3. Add the appropriate acronym for any doctorate-level degrees you have been awarded by accredited educational institutions (for example, Ph.D. for Doctor of Philosophy), but not degrees at the master's level or below, unless you are in the education field.

4. Provide your complete mailing address. Position this information one space below your name, on the left-hand side of your resume. Put your street address on one line; the city, state, and zip on a second, as follows:

4451 Elm Street

Andover, MA 02158

5. If possible, provide two methods by which an employer or recruiter can contact you. Position this information one space below your name, on the right-hand side of your resume. Place the preferred method first and the backup method directly below it, so that the contact information looks like this:

day — (203) 659-2136

Sam@erols.com

Contact methods include (in order of their effectiveness):

A private daytime telephone number that you answer

A private e-mail address that you can check during the day

A private daytime telephone number that another adult answers

A nighttime telephone number that you answer

A private e-mail address that you can check at night

Profile

1. Review your employment materials and identify 3–5 key attributes or qualifications that best support your objective statement. These capabilities usually are your strongest credentials for the job you seek.

2. Check recruitment ads, job postings on the Internet, and position descriptions, if you have access to them, to determine the terms typically used by employers to express your key credentials.

3. Using the words and phrases favored by employers and recruiters, summarize your qualifications in 3–5 bullets or short phrases.

Education

1. List the education degrees you have earned, using the following format: degree/major, educational institution, location, year awarded.

2. List any certificates you have been awarded, using the following format: certificate, certifying organization, year awarded.

3. List major training programs you have completed, using the following format: training program, training organization, year completed.

4. List any educational course or training programs in which you are currently enrolled, citing the course or program, the institution or training organization that is providing it, and the term "ongoing."

Professional affiliations & awards

1. List any professional societies or associations in which you are a member and/or have held an elected or appointed position. Begin with the term *Member* or the name of the position held and then identify the organization by its complete name.

2. List any license you have earned from a state licensing board, using the following format: License name and number, granting organization, year awarded.

3. List any awards you have received from professional societies or associations or from your employer, using the following format: Name or brief description of the award, organization that granted it, year it was presented.

4. List any conference presentation you have made, paper you have had published, or program you have helped organize, using the following format: Title of the presentation or paper, meeting or publication name, date.

Your current or most recent employer

1. State your employer's name and location and your dates of employment on one line, followed by the title of the position you held on the next line. Put your position title in bold.

ADEMCo Enterprises   Malden, MA
1991–Present

Project Manager

2. Use action verbs (such as completed, directed, developed, conducted) and short, but complete sentences to describe your principal tasks in this position. Limit the information you present to a paragraph of no more than 4–5 lines in length. Focus on activities that support your objective and illustrate the strengths you highlighted in your profile.

3. Identify 2–3 achievements you accomplished in this position. Clearly relate these achievements to the activities you described in Step 2. Describe them using quantitative measures (for example, money saved, goods sold, profits earned), wherever possible.

All other previously held positions — in reverse chronological order

1. Repeat Steps 1–3 in the previous section for each position in which you've been employed. If you held several different positions in the same organization, describe each separately, including the dates you held the positions, but don't repeat the name of the employing organization. For example:

ADEMCo Enterprises   Malden, MA
1991–Present

Project Manager   **1997–Present**

One-paragraph description of your activities

List of 2–3 accomplishments

Senior Analyst   **1991–1997**

One-paragraph description of your activities

List of 2–3 accomplishments

Formatting Your Chronological Resume

The format of a chronological resume is identical to that of a functional or hybrid resume, except in the experience section. Working in order of time from most recent to most remote historically, the chronological resume style describes your work experience and credentials through a series of position summaries that detail your previous employers, on-the-job activities, and accomplishments. Organize the sections of your resume in this order:

- Contact information
- OBJECTIVE
- PROFILE
- EXPERIENCE
- EDUCATION
- PROFESSIONAL AFFILIATIONS & AWARDS

Except for your contact information, use all capital letters in the title of each section. Position the title by itself at the top of the section, as shown in the resume layout in Figure 4-1.

If your resume runs to a second page, make sure that you include your contact information there, in case one page becomes separated from the other. Position this information at the top, left-hand side of the page, like the following:

Your name

Your daytime telephone number

Page Two

Figures 4-1 and 4-2 illustrate great chronological resumes that put the whole package together.

Figure 4-1: An illustrative chronological resume.

Robert P. Weldon

79 East 19th Street
Los Angeles, CA 90024

day-(213) 756-8902
rpw39@aol.com

PROFILE
- Over 15 years experience in production of television broadcasts, film and video
- Winner of 5 Emmys as producer of Public Broadcasting Service travel specials
- Hands-on knowledge of managing projects from conceptualization to airing
- Experience managing production crews, talent and celebrity guests

EXPERIENCE

Public Broadcasting Service   *Los Angeles, CA*   *1989-Present*
Senior Producer   1991-Present

Recruited and managed a select team of production professionals creating travel documentaries for public broadcast. Oversaw scripting, casting, logistics and production of three major programs per year, ensuring on-time, on-budget completion. Worked with outside creative talent to design innovative show formats and content, breaking new ground in the production of this genre.
- Successfully produced over 25 programs, generating high audience ratings and earning industry recognition
- Managed a multi-project budget of over $5 million per year for 8 years without a single overrun

Associate Producer   1989-1991

Worked with a production team developing new concepts and themes for public interest programming. Assembled an expert advisory board to review and critique potential initiatives. Designed and implemented several test shows to gauge audience appeal of alternative topics and presentation formats. Analyzed response data and formulated recommendations to senior management.
- Identified core program elements for new action-adventure thrust in public broadcasting
- Established objectives, funding requirements and implementation plans for travel documentaries for children

About Kids   *San Diego, CA*   *1981-1989*
Director

Founded this independent film and video production company. Worked with major broadcast and cable television companies nationwide. Produced projects on an array of topics related to child safety, health, development and education. Directed scripting, casting, field production and editing of film programs running from 30 minutes to over 90 minutes in length.
- Built a profitable film production company with revenues in excess of $1 million per year
- Produced over 8 shows per year without a single budget overrun
- Show entitled "Kid's Treat" was recognized by the U.S. Department of Education for its innovative presentation of dental care for children

EDUCATION
BA/Communications Manhattanville College, Purchase, NY 1980

PROFESSIONAL AFFILIATIONS & AWARDS
5 Emmy Awards National Academy of Television Arts & Sciences 1993-Present
Member National Academy of Television Arts & Sciences
Member Directors Guild of America

Figure 4-2:   A second illustrative chronological resume.

Jennifer A. Logan

56 Holly Leaf Drive   evening-(703) 897-8921
McLean, VA 22102   jennl@erols.com

PROFILE
- 12-year career of success in sales and marketing
- Experienced in building and managing customer relationships
- Track record of achieving year-to-year increases in revenue and profitability
- Solid background in sales and marketing management software programs and Internet applications

EXPERIENCE

Redmont Mutual Assurance Corporation   ***Manassas Park, VA***   ***1995-Present***
District Sales Manager

Organized new sales territory in northern Virginia. Conceived a plan for sales force recruitment and training, product introduction and business development, distribution channel management and promotion. Sold the plan with supporting budget and corporate support commitment to senior management. Executed the plan to drive growth, outpace the competition and achieve rapid return on investment.
- Beat sales target by 30% in first year of operation
- Won 1998 Leadership Merit Award, Redmont's highest marketing honor
- Expanded sales force to 25 agents in 18 months
- Doubled the territory's new accounts and increased sales per account in second year

Edderton Insurance Group   ***Charlottesville, VA***   ***1989-1995***
Territorial Sales Manager

Focused efforts on recruitment, training and support of independent sales agents marketing insurance products to commercial and large industrial accounts. Concurrently, launched new products and developed field support to enhance revenue performance and bottom-line profitability. Installed new sales lead tracking and management system which improved coordination among agents and responsiveness to customers.
- Won first annual Top of the Heap award for district leadership
- Built territory to 50+ agents within 3 years
- Appointed to Special Task Force to design "Territory of the Future"

Industrial Insurance Applications Corporation   ***Charlottesville, VA***   ***1981-1989***
Commercial Underwriting Manager

Built a 6-person underwriting unit into one of the most productive and efficient operations in the company. Directed daily underwriting operations, long range business planning and all training for newly-hired professional staff. Produced quarterly reports for profit and loss assessment and business management by the Executive Committee and Board of directors.
- Implemented supplemental educational program for new actuaries that produced passing scores on every actuarial exam taken for three years running
- Created a new software application for actuarial analysis and long-range planning that improved precision of corporate decision-making

Jennifer A. Logan
(703) 897-8921
Page Two

Ducketsville Insurance Group   ***Charlottesville, VA***   ***1979-1981***
Field Marketing Representative
Managed field sales and marketing programs throughout central Virginia. Developed new client leads, established and maintained contact with prospective clients and managed the start-up of new accounts.
   • Consistently ranked in top 10% of active field agents in the company

EDUCATION
BS/Business Administration   Virginia Tech University, Blacksburg, VA   1979

PROFESSIONAL AFFILIATIONS & AWARDS
   Completed 4 qualifying exams   American Actuarial Association   Ongoing
   Member   American Actuarial Association
   Member   American Marketing Association

CHAPTER 5

WRITING A FUNCTIONAL RESUME

IN THIS CHAPTER

- Making sure a functional resume is best for you
- Getting the content right
- Getting the format right

A functional resume presents your primary occupational competencies, beginning with your area of greatest expertise. It describes each of these workplace skills and abilities, illustrates your experience in using them on the job, and details the results you achieved — all benefits if you are in a technical field or you have a general or managerial background and a career path with one or more breaks.

Deciding to Use a Functional Resume

Understanding a functional resume's strengths and limitations can help you determine whether this format is a good match with your background and ambitions.

Citing the strengths

A functional resume works well if you want to

- **Highlight what you can do and how well you can do it.** The functional resume helps you illustrate your potential to a prospective employer by showing how you applied skills and abilities in prior jobs.

■ **Present your qualifications according to your level of expertise.** By organizing your employment information based on your performance at work, you can focus on your record of actual achievement rather on the time you spent in prior positions.

■ **Effectively describe a nontraditional career path.** The functional resume concentrates on the skills you have acquired and applied regardless of the type and sequence of jobs you've held.

Looking at the limitations

To fully appreciate the functional resume's possible place in your job-search efforts, you need to consider a few drawbacks. This style of resume may

■ **Make it difficult for employers to evaluate your work record.** By omitting your employment history, the functional resume forces employers to sift through a less structured presentation of your prior work to gauge the level of professional competency and success.

■ **Be tough to write because you must synthesize your record into skill areas.** Rather than depend on an orderly record of your work history, the functional resume requires that you look across all your employment experiences to identify and describe your strongest skills and abilities.

■ **Obscure organizational advancement.** Because it focuses on your skills and abilities, a functional resume doesn't provide the framework for demonstrating your steady progress through ever-increasing responsibility throughout your career history.

Weighing these factors, you can see that a functional resume may serve you well if you've developed an array of different skills, worked in a variety of unrelated positions, or if you seek to change careers. This sort of presentation probably is not your best choice if your career has progressed through a traditional path of sustained advancement in a particular field or industry.

Knowing where to start — and how to carry through

Preparing a resume of any type can seem like a formidable task at first, but by following this seven-step process you can put together a winning presentation of your skills and abilities. To develop your functional resume, complete this plan:

1. Collect your employment information. Include any position descriptions and recruitment ads for your previous or current jobs, performance appraisals, project or work descriptions, awards and other professional recognition (for example, certificates of achievement for project contributions), educational record and certificates of completion for training programs, and materials describing your affiliation and participation with professional organizations.

2. Organize your materials according to the skills you are/were able to apply on-the-job, beginning with the skill in which you've gained the highest level of expertise.

3. Prioritize the materials. Use your objective statement to determine three categories of information:

   Critical to supporting your objective and must be included

   Helpful in supporting your objective and should be included if space permits

   Not essential in supporting your objective and can be omitted

4. Write a first draft of your resume. See the next section for details on developing the content and format of your functional resume.

5. Revise your draft. Modify the information you've presented and, if necessary, delete selected segments in order to achieve a maximum length of two pages. Limit deletions to that information you judge to be helpful but not critical to supporting your objective.

6. Edit your draft. Carefully review your draft for misspellings and grammatical, typographical, and other errors. Then ask a friend to review the document to ensure that you have not overlooked any errors and that all the information is easily read and understood.

7. Produce your resume, using either a laser printer or the services of a professional print shop. Use a font size of 11–12 points, high-quality white paper, and black ink. Print each page on a separate sheet of paper rather than on the front and back of the same page.

Developing the Content of Your Functional Resume

The following step-by-step checklist is a helpful aid for developing a great functional resume. Build your contact information, profile, education, and professional affiliations and awards sections first, then develop the all-important experience section. If you need additional information on the basic elements of any good resume, refer to Chapter 2.

Contact information

1. Center your full name at the top of the page and highlight it by putting it in boldface type and possibly using a larger font size (such as 14 points) than the rest of your resume text. Include your middle initial, if appropriate, but not your middle name, unless you use it at work.

2. After your name, add the appropriate acronym for any certifications you have received from recognized independent certifying organizations (for example, CPA for Certified Public Accountant).

3. After your name or certification, add the appropriate acronym for any doctorate-level degrees you have been awarded by accredited educational institutions (such as Ph.D. for Doctor of Philosophy), but not degrees at the master's level (unless you are in the field of education) or below (for example, B.A., A.A.).

4. Provide your complete mailing address. Position this information one space below your name, on the left-hand side of your resume. Put your street address on one line; the city, state, and zip on a second, as follows.

4451 Elm Street

Andover, MA 02158

5. Provide two ways for an employer or recruiter to contact you. Position this information one space below your name, on the right-hand side of your resume. Place the preferred method first and the backup method directly below it, as shown in this example:

day — (203) 659-2136

Sam@erols.com

Contact methods include (in order of their effectiveness):

A private daytime telephone number that you answer

A private e-mail address that you can check during the day

A private daytime telephone number that another adult answers

A nighttime telephone number that you answer

A private e-mail address that you can check at night

Profile

1. Review your employment materials and identify 3–5 key attributes or qualifications that best support your objective statement. These capabilities normally are your strongest credentials for the job you seek.

2. Check recruitment ads, job postings on the Internet, and position descriptions, if you have access to them, to determine the terms typically used by employers to express your key qualifications.

3. As shown later in Figure 5-1, use the words and phrases favored by employers and recruiters to summarize your qualifications in 3–5 bullets or short phrases.

Experience

Beginning with your greatest level of expertise:

1. Identify the skill in which you have the greatest level of expertise using a term or phrase familiar to employers and recruiters. If you included the skill in your profile, repeat the term or phrase you used there. Otherwise, check recruitment ads, job postings on the Internet, and position descriptions, if you have access to them, to determine the term or phrase typically used by employers to express this skill.

2. Describe the skill area by detailing the tasks you performed in various work situations and what outcomes you were able to achieve as a result. Focus on activities that support your objective and illustrate the strengths you highlighted in your profile. Use action verbs and short, but complete sentences. If possible, limit the information you present to a series of 4–5 bullets or a paragraph of similar length. Put the name of the skill in bold.

3. Identify 2–3 of your accomplishments in this skill area. Clearly relate these accomplishments to the activities you describe in the previous step. Wherever possible, describe your results in quantitative measures, such as money saved, goods sold, profits earned, as in the following example:

Achieved revenue growth of 300% in three years

Increased brand recognition and stature by introducing distinctive value-added services

Built company into a regional leader in a highly competitive market

Repeat the steps in the previous section for each of your skill areas. If possible, avoid repeating information in the descriptions of your various skills — using the same examples for every skill is likely to signal limited experience with a range of accomplishments. In every case, however, be complete, detailed, and persuasive.

Education

1. List the education degrees you have earned, using the following format: degree/major, educational institution, location, year awarded.

2. List any certificates you have been awarded, using the following format: certificate, certifying organization, year awarded.

3. List major training programs you have completed, using the following format: training program, training organization, year completed.

4. List any educational course or training programs in which you are currently enrolled, citing the course or program, the institution or training organization which is providing it, and the term "ongoing."

Professional affiliations & awards

1. List any professional societies or associations in which you are a member and/or have held an elected or appointed position. Begin with the term "Member" or the name of the position you held (for example, Program Committee Chair) and then identify the organization by its complete name.

2. List any license you have earned from a state licensing board, using the following format: License name and number, granting organization, year awarded.

3. List any awards you have received from professional societies or associations or from your employer, using the following format: Name/brief description of the award, organization that granted it, year it was presented.

4. List any conference presentation you have made, paper you've published, or program you have helped to organize, using the following format: Title of the presentation or paper, name of the meeting at which it was presented or the publication in which it appeared, date.

Formatting Your Functional Resume

The format of a functional resume is identical to that of a chronological or hybrid resume, except in the experience section, where, in this style, you describe your work experience and credentials through a series of skill summaries organized by level of expertise. Each summary details your use of that skill in various positions and the results you achieved.

Organize the sections of your resume into six key areas. Begin each section, except your contact information, with a title presented in all capital letters and positioned by itself at the top of the section, as shown in Figure 5-1. Here are the sections, in the proper order:

Contact information

OBJECTIVE

PROFILE

EXPERIENCE

EDUCATION

PROFESSIONAL AFFILIATIONS & AWARDS

If you prepare a two-page resume, make sure to include your contact information on the second page in case it becomes separated from the first. Position this information at the top, left-hand side of the page, as shown in the following:

- Your name
- Your daytime telephone number
- Page Two

Figures 5-1 and 5-2 show examples of functional resumes that can share information and attract attention for job seekers who want to either advance their careers or explore entirely new paths.

Figure 5-1:   An illustrative functional resume.

Alan T. Jones

54 Guardian Circle   day-(208) 775-6792
Ithaca, NY 14850   night-(208) 453-8726

OBJECTIVE
An administrative management position with a local municipality where I can deliver
improved operating results at reduced costs.

PROFILE
Twenty-two years of leadership in facilities management. Hands-on experience in
planning, programming and budgeting for large-scale operations. Impeccable record in
purchasing management, achieving significant savings, reduced waste and improved
organizational performance. Caring leader who supports the growth and development of
subordinates.

EXPERIENCE
Facilities Management
- Consolidated inventory of supplies and equipment yielding a 17% reduction in
  storage space requirements and a cost savings of over $50,000 per year
- Planned, organized and successfully executed a physical relocation of 50 employees
  and equipment resulting in minimal disruption to service and genuine improvements
  in work flow
- Supervised 10-person staff providing plumbing, electrical, water and sewer services
  to a residential community of 350

Purchasing Management
- Identified requirements for supplies and equipment, solicited vendors, negotiated
  with selected sources to acquire necessary support on time and below budget
- Developed procedures to identify and acquire "best value" services and products
  reducing customer wait time from five to three days
- Implemented a follow-up quality assurance program to monitor product/service
  performance in an installed environment, reducing customer problems and
  complaints

Staff Leadership and Development
- Assessed staff workload, identified unrealistic requirements, obtained new position
  approvals and recruited and trained new staff to ensure optimum performance and
  high morale
- Managed reorganization that eliminated duplicate positions and reassigned staff into
  more productive and challenging opportunities
- Instituted "open door" policy and resolved personnel issues
- Implemented flexible work schedules to accommodate on-the-job education and
  employee development of workplace skills and knowledge

EDUCATION
BS/Engineering   North Carolina State University, Raleigh, NC   1977

PROFESSIONAL AFFILIATIONS & AWARDS
Member   Logistics Management Institute
Member   National Society of Professional Engineers (NSPE)
"Reducing Cycle Time"   Presented at NSPE Annual Conference   1989
Member   NSPE Kids in Need Program

Figure 5-2:   A second illustrative functional resume.

Patrick O'Shay

8724 Deville Avenue
Detroit, MI 48236

day-(313) 982-8902
paddyo@msn.com

PROFILE
- Planning and Coordinating
- Public Relations and Image Building
- Communications

EXPERIENCE

Planning and Coordinating
Organized and executed large fund-raising projects for both for-profit and not-for-profit organizations. Designed and implemented membership development campaigns. Chaired voluntary programs. Worked with large and small groups to achieve objectives on time and within budget.
- Raised almost $1 million for a healthcare program treating at-risk children
- Invigorated volunteer staff of a start-up professional association, leading to increased membership, participation and dues revenue
- Directed United Way program for a large, multi-state corporation, coordinating separate state-based campaigns and increasing pledges by 14%

Public Relations & Image Building
Developed public relations program to attract new members to professional association. Coordinated media outreach to enhance public image and stature of the organization. Designed, developed and produced an array of promotional literature, including print, video and computer diskette.
- Increased association's membership by 16% in first year and 19% in the following year
- Dramatically expanded brand recognition among key populations, according to focus group testing and surveys
- Increased mentions in the public media by 100%

Communications
Delivered numerous presentations and speeches to a variety of audiences. Appeared on local and national television and radio programs. Chaired meetings and coordinated activities of diverse groups and activities.
- Appeared as a frequent guest on #1-rated television channel in its market
- Received consistently high marks from audiences at national conventions

EDUCATION
BA/English Literature Johns Hopkins University 1979

PROFESSIONAL AFFILIATIONS & AWARDS
Board of Directors Put Hope First Foundation
Member American Society of Association Executives

CHAPTER 6

WRITING A HYBRID RESUME

IN THIS CHAPTER

- Making sure a hybrid resume is best for you
- Getting the content right
- Getting the format right

A hybrid resume contains elements of both a chronological and a functional resume. It presents your primary occupational competencies — beginning with your area of greatest expertise, along with a history of your employment record — beginning with your most recent position. A hybrid resume

- Describes each of your workplace skills and abilities
- Illustrates your experience in using these skills on the job
- Details the results you achieved
- Identifies the title of each position you held, the organization that employed you, the dates you held the positions, and the tasks you performed

Using a Hybrid Resume to Your Advantage

As I note in Chapter 3, a hybrid resume normally works best if you have enjoyed an uninterrupted career in a technical field. Even if that's your background, however, you should confirm that this format is right for you by evaluating its strengths and limitations.

Featuring the strengths

A hybrid resume may be the right choice if you want a document that

■ **Highlights what you can do and how well you can do it.** As with a functional resume, the hybrid format enables you to demonstrate the contribution you can make by describing how you applied specific skills and abilities in your prior jobs.

■ **Enables you to present your qualifications according to your level of expertise.** The hybrid resume ensures that you lead with your strengths by organizing your employment information based on your level of expertise as well as on your record of progression through a series of jobs. As shown in Figure 6-1, a hybrid resume describes both your functional capabilities and your work history.

■ **Is easy to read and understand.** Recruiters can quickly determine what you have done in your career, the industries in which you have had experience, and the kinds of organizations for which you have worked.

■ **Emphasizes continuous progression.** As with a chronological resume, the hybrid format effectively describes a record of steady development by presenting your work experience as a series of positions organized by date.

Sizing up the limitations

When considering whether a hybrid resume might work for you, keep in mind that this format

■ **Often does not provide an adequate description of either your work record or your qualifications.** By including both chronological and functional information, the hybrid format may not have the necessary space to describe either your employment history or your functional expertise completely within the desired two-page length.

■ **May be uncomfortable for some employers and recruiters.** Because it synthesizes the information contained in both a chronological and a functional resume, the hybrid format isn't like most resumes, making it more difficult for employers and recruiters to understand.

A hybrid resume best serves those applicants who have a tightly focused set of skills or who want to emphasize achievements at work more than the positions held. You probably want to choose a different format if you have progressed through a series of increasingly responsible positions, developed an array of different skills, or worked in a variety of unrelated positions.

Building a hybrid resume step-by-step

To develop your hybrid resume, use the following seven-step process:

1. Collect your employment information. Include any position descriptions and recruitment ads for your previous or current jobs, performance appraisals, project or work descriptions, awards and other professional recognition (such as certificate of achievement for project contributions), educational record and certificates of completion for training programs, and materials describing your affiliation and participation with professional organizations.

2. Organize your materials according to the skills you are/were able to apply on the job, beginning with the skill in which you have the highest level of expertise, and their chronology, beginning with your most recent position and working back to your first job.

3. Prioritize the materials. Use your objective statement to determine three categories of information:

Critical to supporting your objective and must be included

Helpful in supporting your objective and should be included if space permits

Not essential in supporting your objective and can be omitted

4. Write a first draft of your resume. See the detailed instructions for developing the content and format of your hybrid resume in the next section.

5. Revise your draft. Modify the information and, if necessary, delete selected segments in order to achieve a maximum length of two pages. Limit deletions to that information you judge to be helpful but not critical to supporting your objective statement.

6. Edit your draft. Carefully review your draft for misspellings and grammatical, typographical, and other errors. Then ask a friend to review the document to ensure that you have not overlooked any errors and that the information is easily read and understood.

7. Produce your resume. Print your resume using a laser printer or have it reproduced at a professional print shop. Use a font size of 11–12 points, high-quality white paper, and black ink. Print each page on a separate sheet of paper rather than on the front and back of the same page.

Closing in on Content

Use the following checklist to develop a great hybrid resume. Build your contact information and profile, education, and professional affiliations and awards sections first, and then develop the all-important Experience section. Chapter 2 can provide additional information about the individual elements in a resume.

Contact information

1. Center your complete name at the top of the page and highlight it by using boldface type and possibly using a larger font size — such as 14 points — than the rest of your resume text. Include your middle initial, if appropriate, but not your middle name, unless you use it at work.

2. After your name, add the appropriate acronym for any certifications you have received from recognized independent certifying organizations (for example, CPA for Certified Public Accountant).

3. After your name, add the appropriate acronym for any doctorate-level degrees you have been awarded by accredited educational institutions (for example, Ph.D. for Doctor of Philosophy), but not degrees at the master's level (unless you are in the field of education) or below (for example, B.A., A.A.).

4. Provide your complete mailing address. Position this information one space below your name, on the left-hand side of your resume. Put your street address on one line and the city, state, and zip on a second, as shown in the following example:

    4451 Elm Street

    Andover, MA 02158

5. Provide two methods by which an employer or recruiter can contact you. Position this information one space below your name, on the right-hand side of your resume. Place the preferred method first and the backup method directly below it, as shown here:

day — (203) 659-2136

Sam@erols.com

Contact methods include (in order of their effectiveness):

A private daytime telephone number that you answer

A private e-mail address that you can check during the day

A private daytime telephone number that another adult answers

A nighttime telephone number that you answer

A private e-mail address that you can check at night

Profile

1. Review your employment materials and identify 3–5 key attributes or qualifications that best support your objective statement. These capabilities normally are your strongest credentials for the job you seek.

2. Check recruitment ads, job postings on the Internet, and position descriptions, if you have access to them, to determine the terms typically used by employers to express your key credentials.

3. Using the words and phrases favored by employers and recruiters, summarize your qualifications in 3–5 bullets or short phrases.

Experience

1. Identify the skill in which you have the greatest level of expertise using a term or phrase that is familiar to employers and recruiters. If you include the skill in your profile, repeat the term or phrase you use there. Otherwise, check recruitment ads, job postings on the

Internet, and position descriptions, if you have access to them, to determine the term or phrase typically used by employers to express this skill.

2. Describe the skill area by detailing the tasks you performed in various work situations and what outcomes you were able to achieve as a result. Focus on activities that support your objective and illustrate the strengths you highlight in your profile. Use action verbs and short but complete sentences. If possible, limit the information you present to a series of 4–5 bullets or a paragraph of similar length. Put the name of the skill in bold, as in this example:

Marketing Program Design & Execution

Pioneered the introduction of conventional marketing concepts into nontraditional markets. Conceptualized, implemented, and managed all aspects of the marketing program to include market research, brand development, service positioning, and client communications.

3. Identify 2–3 of your accomplishments in this skill area. Clearly relate these accomplishments to the activities you described in the paragraph in Step 2. Whenever possible, describe achievements using quantitative measures, such as, money saved, goods sold, profits earned, as in the following examples:

Achieved revenue growth of 300% in three years

Increased brand recognition and stature by introducing distinctive value-added services

Built company into a regional leader in a highly competitive market

Organizing your skills according to your level of expertise, repeat Steps 1–3 for each area of competence. If possible, avoid repeating information — such as using the same examples — in the descriptions of your various skills. In every case, be complete, detailed, and persuasive.

Employment chronology

Beginning with your current or most recent employment situation, state the title of each position, followed by your employer's name, location, and your dates of employment on a separate line. Put each position title in bold. For example:

Project Manager ADEMCo Enterprises Malden, MA 1991–Present

Education

1. List the education degrees you have earned, using the following format: degree/major, educational institution, location, year awarded.

2. List any certificates you have been awarded, using the following format: certificate, certifying organization, year awarded.

3. List major training programs you have completed, using the following format: training program, training organization, year completed.

4. List any educational course or training programs in which you are currently enrolled, citing the course or program, the institution or training organization providing it, and the term "ongoing."

Professional affiliations & awards

1. List any professional societies or associations in which you are a member and/or have held an elected or appointed position. Begin with the term "Member" or the title of the position you held (for example, Program Committee Chair) and then identify the organization by its complete name.

2. List any license you have earned from a state licensing board, using the following format: License name and number, granting organization, year awarded.

3. List any awards you have received from professional societies or associations or from your employer, using this format: Name/brief description of the award, organization that granted it, year it was presented.

4. List any conference presentation you have made, paper you have had published, or program you have helped to organize, using the following format: Title of the presentation or paper, name of the meeting at which it was presented or the publication in which it appeared, date of presentation or publication.

Formatting Your Hybrid Resume

The format of a hybrid resume is identical to that of a chronological or functional resume, except in the experience section. This section in a hybrid format describes your work experience and credentials in two separate subsections: a series of skill summaries organized according to your level of expertise, followed by a list of your prior positions and employers, in reverse chronological order. The list starts out looking like this (note the centering and underlining of "Employment Chronology"):

Contact information

OBJECTIVE

PROFILE

EXPERIENCE

Employment Chronology

EDUCATION

PROFESSIONAL AFFILIATIONS & AWARDS

Begin each section, except your contact information, with a title presented in all caps and positioned by itself at the top of the section, as shown in Figure 6-1. If your resume runs to a second page, make sure that you include your contact information there as well, in case the pages are separated. Position this information at the top, left-hand side of the page, as follows:

Your name

Your daytime telephone number

Page Two

Figures 6-1 and 6-2 are great hybrid resumes that put it all together.

Figure 6-1: An illustrative hybrid resume.

Jill Ste. Pierre

4534 Jensen Boulevard
Washington, D.C. 20420

day-(202) 554-6979
jsp@msn.com

PROFILE
- General management & multi-site operations
- Recruitment & training of staff
- Marketing communications & business presentations

EXPERIENCE

General Management & Multi-Site Operations

Twenty plus years of experience in budgeting, planning, staffing, marketing and directing multi-staff operations generating over $45 million in revenues and consistently high profits. Full P&L responsibility for 15 sites in 6 states. Led team of 11 management personnel and 575 staff. Promoted rapidly throughout career based on success in improving bottom-line financial results, strengthening line management and field support teams and achieving performance goals.

- Consistently achieved or surpassed all revenue, profit and margin improvement objectives
- Introduced standardized business reporting and accounting practices that reduced errors by 15%
- Revitalized and enhanced customer service procedures resulting in 22% gain in repeat business
- Pioneered innovative organizational change initiatives that produced an 18% improvement in performance ratings
- Built new venture from concept to $7+ million in revenues within first year of operation

Recruitment & Training of Staff

Innovative business leader who recognizes the importance of recruiting and developing talent for her organization. Oversaw the design and implementation of aggressive sourcing programs to identify and recruit leading candidates for employment. Provided funding and support for in-house employee "university," to deliver high quality, convenient skills training in an array of technical and workplace skills.

- Approved and funded a 15-module, 2-week training program resulting in a 43% increase in certification among nonexempt personnel
- Slashed 85% of external training budget through implementation of in-house, volunteer peer-to-peer training programs
- Negotiated site contracts that decreased overhead costs by 15%

Marketing Communications & Business Presentations

Conceived, wrote, produced and delivered hundreds of presentations to executives, line managers and field staff. Led effort to reformulate brand and reposition company in the marketplace. Built entire public communications strategy for new brand introduction. Designed and oversaw production of consumer-based marketing promotions and ad campaigns.

- Successfully established a new brand identity for the company
- Focus-group testing indicated a new and higher level of public awareness for the company's products and services

Jill Ste. Pierre
(202) 554-6979
Page Two

Employment Chronology

Management Consultant McLean, VA 1989-Present
Director/Division Manager/District Manager Motel 1 Group, Washington, D.C.
1981-1989
Business Manager Marriott International, Rockville, MD 1977-1981
Marketing Manager Jefferson Commercial Real Estate, Arlington, VA 1971-1977

EDUCATION
BA/Speech & Communications University of Virginia, Charlottesville, VA 1971
Executive Development Program Darden School of Business, University of Virginia,
Charlottesville, VA 1985
MBA/Marketing American University, Washington, D.C. On-Going

PROFESSIONAL AFFILIATIONS & AWARDS
Member American Management Association

Figure 6-2: A second illustrative hybrid resume.

James X. Stoffard

1775 Alicia Court
Wilmington, NC 28207

day-(704) 843-5746
james249@aol.com

OBJECTIVE
A Vice President of Marketing position where I can implement innovative programs to generate rapid revenue and profit growth for an industry leader.

PROFILE
- Market Research
- Revenue & Profit Growth
- Marketing Campaign Management
- Competitive Analysis
- Customer Relationship Management

EXPERIENCE
Market Research
Founded market research organization and built business to #2 in the region within six years. Pioneered the use of online marketing strategies for an array of commercial products and services. Developed complete marketing programs to include market research, product/service positioning, incentive sales programs, client communications strategies and brand development initiatives.
- Developed profitable new markets for mature products and services
- Increased customer retention and solidified market position by incorporating distinctive value-added components in product sales proposition
- Built company into a regional leader within a highly competitive market

Revenue Growth & Business Development
Developed management team and corporate culture necessary to accelerate revenue growth in an under-performing service business. Built sales team and established incentive program to achieve rapid return to profitability. Negotiated key partnerships and alliances.
- Drove up revenue growth by 200% in four years
- Increased market penetration by creating distinctive selling proposition
- Expanded repeat sales by using technological innovation to enhance client satisfaction

Marketing Campaign Management
Employed proven marketing strategies and techniques to create numerous marketing campaigns. Performed market research, competitive analysis, surveys and personal selling in a sensitive and highly visible public position. Worked with radio, television and print media to craft highly focused and compelling messages.
- Pioneer in the use of database marketing strategies and targeted direct marketing campaigns
- Demonstrated excellence in public speaking and media appearances
- Oversaw ad agency program that was nominated for a national industry award

James X. Stoffard
(704) 843-5746
Page Two

Relationship Management & Client Retention
Established relationship management culture and infrastructure for sales organization. Taught and modeled the concept of "relationships for life," to help sales agents appreciate the importance of long-term client relationships and accept responsibility for them. Created programs to reward both sales agents and customers for sustaining relationships.
- Consistently generated revenues at six times the industry average per client
- Awarded corporate Superior Achievement Commendation
- Reduced cost of new client acquisition by 15%

Employment Chronology

President/COO   Piedmont Marketing Services, Inc., Wilmington, NC   1992-Present
Vice President, Marketing   Beltone Mobile Systems of North Carolina, Wilmington, NC 1977-1992
Marketing Manager   Communications Maintenance Associates, Carmel, CA   1972-1977

EDUCATION
MBA   University of North Carolina, Chapel Hill, NC   1992
BA/Art History   Indiana University, Bloomington, IN   1972

PROFESSIONAL AFFILIATIONS & AWARDS
Participant   Leadership Carolinas
Member   American Marketing Association

CHAPTER 7

WRITING A GREAT RESUME IF YOU'RE LOOKING FOR YOUR FIRST JOB

IN THIS CHAPTER

- Figuring out what counts on your resume
- Creating a resume with all the right stuff
- Organizing your stuff for maximum impact

First-time job seekers are best served by a modified functional resume. This format presents your primary employment capabilities, beginning with your area of greatest expertise. The resume describes each of your workplace skills and abilities and illustrates your experience in using them in both paid employment and in other, unpaid activities.

Gathering Evidence of Your Capabilities

Creating an effective resume begins as a research project. You want to identify and collect all the information that describes the skills and knowledge you've acquired — in school, extracurricular, and other non-work activities and on the job — and any experience you've had in the workplace.

Looking beyond paid employment

If you're a first-time job seeker, your formal employment experience probably is limited to part-time jobs and full-time positions during summer breaks from school. These situations are important because they enable you to demonstrate your skills in a paid work environment. You also can demonstrate your employability by describing your unpaid work in other areas, including internships, school activities, volunteer contributions, and even your hobbies and other interests. The following definitions can help you focus on contributions worthy of a mention in your resume:

- **Internships** include any workplace function or activity performed under the guidance or sponsorship of an academic institution, employer, or other organization.

- **School activities** include any extracurricular programs in which you participated as a student, including student government, clubs, issue advocacy, and athletics.

- **Volunteer work** include any role you had in civic, social, community, or other programs designed to assist, support, or promote specific organizations or causes.

Warning

We live in an imperfect world, and some employers may not appreciate some of the causes and issues you have worked for. Therefore, play it safe and cite only those that aren't controversial or antagonistic to the business community.

- **Hobbies and interests** involve your participation in any group organized by those with similar interests or affinities.

Recognizing your accomplishments

These unpaid work activities enable recruiters and employers to identify your skills and abilities even when you haven't been paid directly for using your time, energy, and talents. Your accomplishments help in the assessment of your level of expertise in those skills and abilities. Accomplishments can include any awards or recognition you received or results you achieved through your participation.

Developing your resume

You can develop your resume by using a seven-step process that begins with gathering the history of your paid and unpaid work experience and proceeds through printing your finished product — one great resume that reflects your history and hopes! Just follow this plan:

1. Collect your employment information. Include any position descriptions and announcements for your previous or current paid and unpaid work, academic and work-related awards and recognition, educational record, and materials describing your affiliation and participation with the student chapters of professional organizations.

2. Organize your materials according to the skills you are/were able to apply in these activities, beginning with the skill in which you have developed the highest level of expertise.

3. Prioritize the materials. Use your objective statement to determine three categories of information:

   Critical to supporting your objective and must be included

   Helpful in supporting your objective and should be included if space permits

   Not essential in supporting your objective and can be omitted

4. Write a first draft of your resume. See the next section for detailed instructions on developing the content and format of your resume.

5. Revise your draft. Modify the information you presented and, if necessary, delete selected segments in order to achieve a maximum length of two pages. Limit deletions to that information you judged to be helpful but not critical to supporting your objective.

6. Edit your draft. Carefully review your draft for misspellings and grammatical, typographical, and other errors. Then, ask a friend to review the document to ensure that you didn't miss any errors and that the information presented is understandable and easy to read.

7. Produce your resume. Print your resume using a laser printer, or have it reproduced at a professional print shop. Use a font size of 11–12 points, high-quality white paper, and black ink. Print each page on a separate sheet of paper rather than on the front and back of the same page.

Developing Your Resume's Content

The following checklist provides a framework for building a great resume, a solid account of your credentials and job-related direction. Build your contact information and profile, education, and professional affiliations and awards sections first, and then develop the all-important experience section. If you need more details on the core elements of a well-designed resume, refer to Chapter 2.

Contact information

1. Center your full name at the top of the page and highlight it by using boldface type and possibly using a larger font size (like 14 points) than the rest of your resume text. Include your middle initial, if appropriate, but not your middle name, unless you use it at work.

2. Provide your complete mailing address. Use an address that won't change for at least six months (for example, because you will be graduating) and where you can check your mail daily. Position this information one space below your name, on the left-hand side of your resume. Put your street address on one line; the city, state, and zip on a second, as follows:

4451 Elm Street

Andover, MA 02158

3. Provide two methods by which an employer or company recruiter can contact you. As with your address, these methods should be effective for at least six months. Position this information one space below your name, on the right-hand side of your resume. Place the preferred method first and the backup method directly below it, as shown here:

day — (203) 659-2136

`Sam@erols.com`

Contact methods include (in order of their effectiveness):

A private daytime telephone number that you answer

A private e-mail address that you can check during the day

A private daytime telephone number that another adult answers

A nighttime telephone number that you answer

A private e-mail address that you can check at night

Profile

1. Review your employment materials and identify 3–5 key attributes or qualifications that best support your objective statement. These capabilities normally are your strongest credentials for the job you seek.

2. Check recruitment ads, job postings on the Internet, and position descriptions, if you have access to them, to determine the terms typically used by employers to express your key qualifications.

3. Using the words and phrases favored by employers and recruiters, summarize your qualifications in 3–5 bullets or short phrases.

Education

1. List the education degrees you have earned or will earn upon graduation, using the following format: degree/major, educational institution, location, year awarded.

2. List any academic awards or scholarships you received and your grade point average if it is equal to a B (3.3 on a 4-point scale) or higher.

3. List any certificates you have been awarded, using the following format: certificate, certifying organization, year awarded.

Experience

1. Identify the skill in which you have the greatest level of expertise, using a term or phrase that is familiar to employers and recruiters. If you have included the skill in your profile, repeat the term or phrase you used there. Otherwise, check recruitment ads, job postings on the Internet, and position descriptions, if you have access to them, to determine the term or phrase typically used by employers to express this skill.

2. Describe the skill area by detailing the tasks you performed in various work situations (unpaid as well as paid) and what outcomes you were able to achieve. Focus on activities that support your objective and illustrate the strengths you highlighted in your profile. Use action verbs and short but complete sentences. If possible, limit the information you present to a series of 4–5 bullets or a paragraph of similar length. Put the name of the skill in bold, as in this example:

Project Management

Chaired a task force for the Student Government Association to identify alternative financing options for on-campus entertainment events. Surveyed leading colleges and universities around the country to determine their methods. Interviewed university's vice president of finance to get his perspective. Developed a slate of options and presented them to the Association's Executive Committee for decision.

3. Identify 2–3 of your accomplishments in this skill area. Clearly relate these accomplishments to the activities you described in Step 2. Wherever possible, describe them using quantitative measures, such as money saved, goods sold, profits earned, as in these examples:

   Completed project two months prior to assigned deadline

   Selected option increased revenues from student programs by 15% in six months

   Personal leadership of the project was recognized in a letter of appreciation from Student Government Association president

Repeat Steps 1–3 for each of your skill areas. If possible, avoid using the same examples in the descriptions of your various skills. In every case, however, be complete, detailed, and persuasive.

Professional affiliations & awards

1. List any professional societies or associations in which you are/were a student member. Begin with the term "Member" and then identify the organization by its complete name.

2. List the student chapter or affiliate of any professional societies or associations in which you have held an elected or appointed position. Begin with the title of the position you held and then identify the organization by its complete name.

3. List any awards you have received from professional societies or associations, using the following format: Name/brief description of the award, organization which granted it, year it was presented.

4. List any conference presentation you have made, paper you have had published, or program you have helped to organize, using the following format: title of the presentation or paper, name of the meeting at which it was presented or the publication in which it appeared, date of presentation or publication.

Formatting Your Resume

A modified version of a standard functional resume is the best format for first-time job seekers. The modification occurs in the experience section. In that section, the resume describes your work experience and credentials through a series of skill summaries organized by your level of expertise. Each summary details your use of that skill in various positions and the results you achieved.

Because you've spent less time in the workplace than those with more experience, your resume leads with your strength. This strength is the exposure your recent education has given you to the latest concepts and knowledge in your field. Therefore, you need to position your education section before that of your work experience in order to highlight this aspect of your qualifications.

You can build a description of your functional expertise by organizing the sections of your resume in the following order:

Contact information

OBJECTIVE

PROFILE

EDUCATION

EXPERIENCE

PROFESSIONAL AFFILIATIONS & AWARDS

Begin each section, except your contact information, with a titl presented in all caps and positioned by itself at the top of the sec tion, as shown in Figure 7-1.

If your resume runs to a second page, make sure that you includ your contact information there, as well, in case one page become separated from the other. Position this information at the top, left hand side of the page, as shown below:

Your name

Your daytime telephone number

Page Two

Figures 7-1 and 7-2 illustrate sample resumes that pull togethe details for a first-time job seeker's venture into the marketplace.

Figure 7-1:   Illustrative first-time job seeker resume.

Clifford R. Early

15 Ophelia Hall
Medford, MA 02121

day-(617) 838-9825
cliffe@tufts.edu

OBJECTIVE
A systems engineering position with a cutting edge company where I can apply my education to help create state-of-the-art products.

PROFILE
- Application oriented
- Schooled and practiced in experimental and analytical methods
- Demonstrated ability to collaborate with and lead project teams
- Modeling, control, and integration of dissimilar technologies

EDUCATION
MS/Computer & Systems Engineering Tufts University, Medford, MA   4.0/4.0
Expected, May 1999
BS/Electrical Engineering Rochester Polytechnic Institute, Troy, NY Cum Laude
1997

EXPERIENCE
Control System Design & Analysis
- Classical control, notably root-locus, and bode design methods
- Multiple input, multiple output state space analysis
- System identification techniques applied to bulk forming
- Path planning optimization development for manufacturing processes
- Control system design and analysis for structural compensation

System Modeling
- Frequency and time domain, input-output and state space, nonlinear methods, Monte-Carlo and probabilistic analyses, computational and analytic model development
- Deformation modeling based on upper-bound analysis and thermal modeling for real-time control applications
- Electro-hydraulic and direct-drive valves, hydraulic motors and rams
- Lasers, detectors, molecular filters, scattering and performance, power and noise modeling for velocity sensing

System Design and Testing
- Architecture design and development
- Hardware and software partitioning issues
- System performance testing
- Failure detection, isolation, and correction

Clifford R. Early
(617) 838-9825
Page Two

Electronic & Instrumentation Design
- Analog electronics design
- Servo loops
- High-frequency amplifiers
- Data acquisition system development
- Extrusion press sensor integration
- State machines
- Programmable logic devices
- Computer interfaces

Leadership
- Participated in and led project teams
- Defined and planned new projects
- Teach and mentor undergraduate students

PROFESSIONAL AFFILIATIONS & AWARDS
Member   Tau Beta Pi Honor Society
Member   IEEE Control Systems Society
"Application of Modeling Techniques to Structural Integrity Problems" with Andus
Freinze, presented at 7th IEEE Conference on Control Applications, Orlando, FL   1998

Figure 7-2:   Another illustrative first-time job seeker resume.

Richard Johnson

1819 Altine Avenue   day-(805) 891-7690
Westlake Village, CA 91361   pager-(888) 555-2682

PROFILE
- Management and supervision
- Financial administration
- Data systems operation

EDUCATION
BA/Business Administration   California State University, Long Beach, CA
Expected, June, 1999

EXPERIENCE
Management and Supervision
While still a full-time student, supervised a grocer's night shift of 12 employees. Directed
operations involving logistics, maintenance, security, product control, and quality
assurance. Trained new employees.
- One of this retail grocery chain's youngest supervisors
- Earned superior ratings from Store Manager
- Worked effectively with people of all ethnic backgrounds and ages

Financial Administration
Performed accounts payable function for University library. Logged in all
correspondence. Scheduled invoices for payment. Answered inquiries from vendors
and supported Comptroller with special projects.
- Improved filing system and reduced errors in accounts payable administration
- Given increased responsibilities based on superior performance
- Gained in-depth knowledge of financial management software programs

Data Systems Operation
Selected for student financial aid position in University Computer Operations Department.
Quickly learned all data entry procedures and performed assigned tasks with a minimum
of supervision. Learned PC applications, including Windows Excel and Access.
- Recognized by department manager for on-time, error-free performance

PROFESSIONAL AFFILIATIONS & AWARDS
Member   Student Chapter, AICPA
Member   Student Investing Club

CHAPTER 8

WRITING AN ELECTRONIC RESUME

IN THIS CHAPTER

- Addressing the new technology in HR departments
- Creating a state-of-the-art version of your resume
- Getting your state-of-the-art resume onto paper

Today, a great resume is one that describes your employment credentials with clarity and power, and presents that information in a format that's compatible with the advanced technology now being used by many human resource departments.

Understanding the State-of-the-Art HR Department

A quiet but pervasive technological revolution has occurred in the human resource departments of both for-profit corporations and nonprofit organizations in the United States.

Understanding the role of scanners and computers

In the past, human resource departments largely worked with paper. They used paper resumes to evaluate candidates for their current openings and paper files to store those resumes for consideration for future openings. This process worked because the pace of recruiting was relatively relaxed and the number of candidates involved was small.

Today, however, employers face a very different environment:

■ Job openings occur much more frequently and in much larger numbers as organizations continually shift their product and service strategies, facility locations, and markets.

■ The number of candidates has increased dramatically as more individuals assume responsibility for managing their own careers. Turnover has also increased as employees leave to take better jobs elsewhere.

■ In order to reduce overhead costs, many companies have downsized their human resource staffs.

■ Senior managers and executives are more aware of the serious impact that unfilled positions can have on an organization's operations and its bottom line.

The net result of these factors has been a fundamental change in the way many HR departments handle resumes. Today, most employers use computer-based resume management systems to accept, process, store, and review these documents.

Computer-based resume management systems typically have three components:

■ **A scanner.** This device uses optical character recognition technology to take a picture of your resume and translate it into information that computers can accept and use.

■ **A computerized database.** This area of the system stores the information contained on resumes so that it can be quickly retrieved for review when needed.

■ **A search engine.** This software application enables recruiters to locate specific resumes in the database that match the requirements for their open positions.

Typically, a resume management system is used in an administrative process, as described in the following sequence:

1. Resumes are received in the HR Department, removed from their envelopes, and quickly evaluated to determine whether they can be scanned.

2. Those resumes that are acceptable are placed in a queue for scanning.

3. Resumes that cannot be scanned are usually discarded, often without any notification of the individuals who sent them.

4. Acceptable resumes are scanned and then input into the computer's database. In most cases, HR departments don't have the staff to review the accuracy of the scanner's copy or to correct any errors it may make.

5. The scanned document is then available for search by recruiters who are seeking candidates for open positions. Recruiters specify key words to the search engine, which searches every word in every resume to identify those documents that contain matching words. The information the selected resumes contain is further reviewed and then a decision is made about each individual's qualifications for the open positions.

Braving the new world of scanners

Every step of the HR screening process contains obstacles for your resume. If you carefully consider these points, your resume has a better chance of making it through the initial stages of processing:

■ If you send your resume to an employer and it is not in a suitable format for scanning, the employer may discard it and you will not be considered for the opportunities available with that employer.

■ If your resume makes it through the scanning process, but contains formatting and other word-processing conventions that are not compatible with the scanner, the resulting computer file may contain numerous errors that will not be detected before it is input into the computer's database.

■ Finally, if the electronic file containing your resume has numerous errors or terms that do not match the keywords that the recruiters use, the search engine will not find any matches in your resume information.

Remember

You may have written a great resume, but if the document's not compatible with the technology in today's HR department, you may be overlooked, even if you are qualified for a particular position.

Not every HR department uses a computer-based resume management system. However, you're not likely to know which do not. Therefore, the safest course is to assume that every employer is using this technology.

What does this assumption mean for your resume? Unless you know for sure that an employer is still relying on a paper-shuffle plan for keeping track of resumes, you need to reconfigure that document into an electronic resume — one that is computer-friendly.

Writing a Computer-Friendly Version of Your Resume

To transform your resume into a document acceptable to computer systems, you have to adjust both its format and content. However, the resulting electronic resume should be appealing for the human recruiter, so that you can use it for all of your job searching and career management requirements.

Adapting your resume to a universal electronic format

Scanners are fickle machines. They are generally reliable when information is presented in a form that they can easily recognize, but are highly unreliable when information appears in other styles or formats. For example, if you emphasize the word *engineer* in your resume by underlining it, most scanners will not be able to read the letters accurately. As a result, the word may be translated into such gibberish as *etttjurrneeet* by the computer, essentially guaranteeing that a keyword search will be unable to match you for an engineer position.

Tip

To ensure that a scanner will read the information on your resume correctly, adhere to the following Do's and Don'ts in formatting your resume:

- **Do** use a font size of 11–12 points. Text this size is large enough for a scanner to read, but doesn't use too much space on your resume.

- **Do** use a typeface that is simple and clean, such as Univers, Times New Roman, or Arial.

- **Do** use bold lettering in moderation. Limit bolding to major organizational headings (such as section titles) and key information that you want to emphasize (such as the titles of positions you've held).

- **Do** use bullets, but ensure that they are solid bullets. Scanners may read open bullets as the letter *o*.

- **Do not** use underlining or italic.

- **Do not** use columns or other landscaping techniques. Scanners read from left to right and often distinguish each column as a separate page of information.

- **Do not** use shading. In order to read a word accurately, scanners need as much contrast as possible between the letters in the word and the background of the page.

■ **Do not** use boxes or other graphics. Scanners often read the vertical line in a box as an "I" and thus completely misread the information it contains.

These guidelines can help to ensure that your resume's information is accurately scanned and input into the database of a computer-based resume management system. And the information that gets put into the database determines whether your resume is ever identified for the kind of job you want.

Reworking your resume content

Computers locate specific resumes stored in their databases by matching the words contained in each resume with keywords that the recruiter specifies. These keywords normally are nouns and phrases that describe the credentials a person must have to be qualified for an open position.

Computers can't read between the lines or draw out clues from other information that your resume contains. Computers can only make comparisons and identify exact matches. For example, if a recruiter uses the keywords "human resources management" as the search criteria, the computer will find any resume with that precise wording, but not any resume in which

■ A term varies even slightly (such as "human resource management")

■ You use a synonym (such as "personnel administration"), even though both terms often are used interchangeably

■ Any misspelled word (such as human resources managfement)

Tip

The key to creating an effective electronic resume is to ensure that you include all the possible key words that recruiters may use to identify a candidate with your qualifications and experience. You also need to be sure that you spell every word on your resume correctly.

How do you determine what keywords recruiters are likely to use? Check out these resources:

- Recruitment ads in newspapers and other publications

- Job postings at employment-related sites on the Internet

- Position descriptions or other documents used in HR departments to detail a job's functions and skills requirements

- Recruiters and human resource professionals you may know or whom you can contact

Identify the most common nouns and phrases HR departments use to describe a candidate who is qualified for a job similar to the one you want. Use their vocabulary to describe your applicable skills, knowledge, and experience. As I note in Chapters 2 and 3, these terms should appear, as appropriate, in every section of your resume, including your objective and profile.

For example, the following job posting is rich in keywords.

Vice President

Manufacturing

Exceptional leadership opportunity for results-focused manufacturing professional to take full P&L responsibility for our multi-plant, mid-south operations. Your experience base should include general management, turnaround, and a record of success in achieving business growth and profit. Career history should reflect progressive management assignments. A solid background in high-volume, metalworking and assembly in a large plant environment essential. Extensive knowledge of manufacturing processes, materials, automation, and cell manufacturing a prerequisite. Skill base should include capital planning, budget and cost controls, labor, overhead, and inventory. Exposure to cast processing a plus. Management style should be take-charge, team-centered, and foster accountability. Bachelor's degree and continuing education required.

Some of the keywords used are:

- Multi-plant operations
- Turnaround experience
- High-volume metal working and assembly
- Large plant environment
- Manufacturing processes, materials, automation
- Cell manufacturing
- Capital budgeting
- Budget and cost controls
- Overhead and inventory
- Cast processing
- Bachelor's degree
- Continuing education

If these terms describe qualifications similar to your own, they would be appropriate keywords to include in your resume.

Producing Your Computer-Friendly Resume

The final production of your resume, as well as the way you deliver the document to employers, can affect how a computer responds to this very important paper (VIP). Factors such as ink, paper color, and paper quality also can have an impact on how well your resume scans.

Selecting paper and ink for your electronic resume

Scanners work best when the words in your resume are in sharp color contrast to the paper on which they are printed. Therefore, avoid using cream or buff paper — although both are often recommended by traditional resume guides — because those colors can diminish the level of contrast between the print and the page. In addition, do not use blue, brown, or other eye-catching ink colors. Instead, stick with black ink and a high grade of bright white paper. The combination may have less visual impact for humans, but scanners love it.

Tip

Make sure that you use a laser or ink jet printer and a fresh ink cartridge to print your resume. Do not use a dot-matrix printer, as many scanners can't read the copies printed with these machines. If you do not have access to a high-grade printer, use a commercial print shop to reproduce your resume.

The right grade of paper is also important. Although formerly fashionable, resumes reproduced on parchment or other heavy grades of paper often cause scanners to choke. To get the best results, use copier (20 lb.) or offset printing (60 lb.) paper. In addition, always use a standard paper size of 8 ½-x-11 inches.

Finally, if your resume runs more than one page in length, use two separate sheets of paper rather than using both sides of the same page. Otherwise, the scanner has to be stopped, your resume retrieved, turned over and run again in order to get both pages of information into the system. That means extra work for the scanner operator, assuming that he or she even notices that your resume is printed on both front and back. The worst consequence, of course, is that only half of your resume is successfully scanned in.

Sending your electronic resume to employers

While poor formatting and content create many of the problems associated with processing resumes through a resume management system, the way you send your resume to an employer can also undermine its effectiveness. Therefore, use the following guidelines when forwarding your document:

- Always send your resume unfolded in a large envelope. The creases created when you fold a resume for a normal #10 business envelope can mar the clarity of the printed text.

- Always paperclip the pages of your resume together. The HR department will separate all pages for scanning, and removing staples can damage your resume and affect its processing.

Transforming your resume into a computer-friendly layout enhances your effectiveness in the job market. The following document shows how you can highlight your employment credentials and enable an employer to input your qualifications accurately into a resume management system.

Your Name

Your street address   Telephone #
Your city, town, zip   E-mail address

OBJECTIVE
Use keywords wherever possible to describe your employment objective and relate it to an employer's requirements and mission.

PROFILE
Use keywords to detail your primary skills, knowledge, abilities, and experience.

EXPERIENCE
Your position title or key skill area
Use skill words and their synonyms in a 4–5 line paragraph that describes what you did in this position or how you demonstrated this skill area at work.

List 1–3 accomplishments, setting each off with a solid bullet.

Your position title or key skill area
Use skill words and their synonyms in a 4–5-line paragraph that describes what you did in this position, or how you demonstrated this skill area at work.

List 1–3 accomplishments, setting each off with a solid bullet.

EDUCATION
List your degrees using the terms most prevalent among recruiters. If space permits, use both the complete name and its acronym — Master's in Business Administration (MBA), for example.

PROFESSIONAL AFFILIATIONS & AWARDS

List your professional activities and awards, using keywords, wherever appropriate.

CHAPTER 9
DEVELOPING AN INTERNET RESUME

IN THIS CHAPTER

- Using the Internet to find a new or great job
- Creating a version of your resume for use online
- Sending your resume over the Internet

According to recent surveys, more than half of all employers and a growing number of staffing firms, employment agencies, and executive recruiters are now using the Internet to identify candidates for open positions. In order to take advantage of these opportunities, however, you must tailor a resume for use on the Internet and know where and how to send it online.

Understanding How Employers and Recruiters Use the Internet

Employers and third-party recruiters — staffing firms and employment agencies — are always seeking quicker, less expensive methods of finding high-quality candidates for their open positions. Traditionally, they have had to rely on relatively expensive print advertisements and time-consuming networking to make these connections. With the advent of the Internet, however, employers and third-party recruiters have a versatile medium that offers them considerable cost and time advantages.

The number of employment-related sites on the Internet and World Wide Web has increased dramatically since the early

1990s. Today, more than 100,000 of these destinations exist, operated by commercial recruitment companies, professional and trade associations, government agencies, and employers themselves. Table 9-1 lists some of the more popular sites, based on their visitor traffic.

Table 9-1: Employment Related Web-Sites

Site Name	Site's Internet Address/URL
America's Job Bank	www.ajb.dni.us
AOL Workplace (click on business/ careers in Web Centers)	www.aol.com
CareerBuilder Network	www.careerbuilder.com
CareerMosaic	www.careermosaic.com
CareerPath.com	www.careerpath.com
Careers.wsj.com	www.careers.wsj.com
Dice	www.dice.com
HeadHunter.Net	www.headhunter.net
HotJobs	www.hotjobs.com
Monster.com	www.monster.com
NationJob, Inc.	www.nationjob.com

Employers use these sites for two purposes: posting announcements of open positions and searching for resumes stored in databases maintained by the sites.

Checking out online job postings

A *job posting* is the electronic equivalent of a classified ad. It describes the skills, knowledge, and experience an employer requires and identifies one or more methods by which you can submit your resume for consideration. In addition, the posting may also provide information about the employer.

A site may have as few as five or six job postings and as many as several hundred thousand. In most cases, and particularly at the larger sites, these openings are stored in a computerized database. They are invisible until you tell the computer the specific kind of job you want. The computer's search engine looks through all the openings stored in its database and lists those that match your criteria. Here's how a job posting may look:

Jacobson & Healey, Inc.

Office Manager/Accounting

Job Location:

McLean, VA

Qualifications:

Minimum of three to four years of experience in a position that relates to Office Management/Accounting. Must have a bachelor's degree with concentration in business and/or accounting. Strong writing and communications skills are necessary. Proficiency in Great Plains accounting software is required.

Duties/Responsibilities:

Manage office operations and oversee employee medical, insurance, and payroll plans. Handle ordering of office supplies, monitor vendor and service contracts, coordinate filing systems, implement office policies and procedures, and oversee postal and delivery functions. Keep general books and records, perform allocations of various expenses, manage bank accounts, and keep detailed ledgers.

Compensation/Benefits:

Salary is $40,000–$50,000, depending on experience and qualifications.

How to Apply:

Please e-mail your resume to `jhi@aol.com`

or

Visit our Web site at `www.jhi-inc.com` for additional information and to apply.

Getting discovered on the Web

Many of the employment-related sites on the Internet maintain databases where you can store your resume for viewing by employers. Although all sites are different, most hold a resume in their databases for 3–12 months, and often permit you to update your employment information at any time during that period.

Storing your resume in an online database is an effective way to put your credentials into circulation. Employers all over the world have access to the document 24 hours a day, 7 days a week. While you're at work or on vacation, your resume is promoting your qualifications to employers who are trying to fill vacant positions. And best of all, you rarely encounter a fee for this service.

Employers, on the other hand, pay either to enter and search the database, or to obtain a candidate's contact information after a person's resume is identified as a match with their requirements for a specific job. Some of these databases contain fewer than 50 resumes, while the larger sites can hold thousands of documents.

Employers search the databases by specifying the knowledge, skills, and experience they seek in a candidate. These search criteria are called *keywords*. The computer reads through every resume in its database and identifies those with terms that match the keywords. The employer can then review each resume and select specific individuals to contact for further evaluation.

Developing an Internet-Ready Version of Your Resume

The Internet is clearly an important way to connect with employers trying to fill their open positions. Your resume is the principal vehicle for making those connections, and you must design it especially to accomplish this task.

In order to respond to the jobs that employers post at employment-related Web sites, your resume has to be able to travel through the Internet. In almost every case, your resume makes this journey in the form of e-mail. However, the technology that makes e-mail messages possible doesn't work well with resumes created with conventional word-processing software. Therefore, to ensure that your resume arrives at its intended destination without being garbled, you need to reconfigure it for e-mail transmission and receipt.

The same requirement also applies when you enter your resume into an online resume database. Although some sites still accept and process paper resumes, most now require that you complete a form provided at their sites or send your resume via e-mail. Further, you may have to revise the content of your resume to ensure that the computer can find it in the database when your qualifications match the requirements for an available position. Otherwise, you will have successfully sent your resume over the Internet, only to have it overlooked after it arrives at its destination.

Revising the format of your resume

The formatting and styles in your conventional resume may look great, but they're not going to survive a trip by e-mail. Creating an Internet resume requires attention to the following four key areas:

- The way information is organized and structured

- The way information is emphasized

- The length of the lines of text in your resume

- The kind of bullets you use to highlight your accomplishments

You first need to alter the way information is organized and structured in your resume. When you create a resume in a word-processing program, you arrange information in paragraphs using indenting, tabs, and other devices to make it more readable. E-mail does not recognize such processing conventions, so you must eliminate them from your resume. To eliminate the formatting in your resume, follow these steps:

1. Open the document on your computer.

2. Click the File function on your toolbar and then click Save As.

3. In the Save As Type drop-down list, select ASCII (American Standard Code for Information Interchange), Text Only, or Rich Text Format.

4. Click Save and your resume will be reproduced as an unformatted page of information. The resulting document doesn't look like much to the human eye, but the Internet loves it.

You also need to alter the way you emphasize the information on your resume. Most people use underlining and boldface type to emphasize certain points on their resumes. But e-mail cannot translate these flourishes, so you need to eliminate them in an Internet resume. To denote emphasis, capitalize all the letters in specific words and phrases.

Don't overuse all caps. In most cases, you should limit all caps to YOUR NAME and the following principal section headings:

- OBJECTIVE

- EXPERIENCE

- PROFILE

- EDUCATION

- PROFESSIONAL AFFILIATIONS & AWARDS

In a chronological and hybrid resume, use all caps for the titles of the positions you've held. In a functional and hybrid resume, capitalize your highlighted skills and abilities.

You should also adjust the length of the lines of text in your resume. Most e-mail readers are set at a width of 60–65 characters. Lines of text that run longer than that are almost always garbled as these readers can't implement the line wrapping function used in word processing systems. To ensure that your text gets read accurately, you must slim down the unformatted version of your resume. Count the characters in each line and insert a hard return — end the line by using the Enter key on your keyboard — at or before the 65-character limit. It's a tedious process and creates an odd-looking document, but by completing this step, you know that your resume can be read by almost all e-mail systems.

And you should be careful about the kind of bullets you use to highlight your accomplishments — e-mail readers don't recognize bullets. Therefore, use the + sign followed by two spaces to create a bullet-like effect on your Internet resume.

For example:

+ Reduced overhead by 24% in less than 18 months

Changing the content of your resume

Your resume's next stop — after safely traveling through the Internet — is likely to be in a computerized database. As with the resume management systems I describe in Chapter 8, these online databases hold information on a wide variety of candidates. To find the resumes of qualified individuals, recruiters must use keywords or search criteria to describe to a search engine the specific characteristics they seek. The search engine probes the database for resumes containing words that match those criteria.

Computers can't read between the lines or make assumptions about information that your resume is missing. Computers can only make comparisons and identify exact matches with the terms that actually appear in the document. For example, if a recruiter uses the keywords "human resources management" as the search criteria, the computer finds any resume with that precise term. The computer won't find resumes with the following conditions:

- Even the most simple variation in the term — "human resource management" for example

- A synonym — "personnel administration" — even though both terms are often used interchangeably

- Any misspelled keywords — "human resources "managfement" for example

Hence, the secret to creating an effective Internet resume is to include all possible keywords that recruiters may use to identify a candidate with your qualifications and experience. You also need to spell all those words correctly. For additional information on how you can identify the best keywords for your resume, see Chapter 8.

Transmitting Your Internet Resume

You can use your Internet resume to respond to job postings at commercial job search Web sites and at an employer's corporate site. You can also use your Internet resume to enter your credentials in one or more online resume databases where employers and third-party recruiters can access them.

Responding to job postings

As you can see in the illustrative job posting for Jacobson & Healey, Inc. in the previous section, most employers want you to send your resume by embedding it in an online application form available at their Web sites or via e-mail.

When including your resume in an online application form, follow the directions the employer provides and carefully proofread the final document before submitting it. When you send your resume by e-mail, always use the Internet version of that document and follow this three-step process:

1. Address your message exactly as directed in the posting. Identify the position in the subject line, using either its designated requisition number or the position title the employer uses in the posting.

2. Cut and paste your resume into the body of the e-mail message, using the appropriate functions on your computer's toolbar.

   It's best not to send your resume as an attachment. Most human resources departments do not open attachments because they are the principal way computer viruses are spread over the Internet. Hence, HR staffs normally delete messages with attachments without notifying the sender.

3. Proofread your message. It's actually best to perform two checks before you send your message. First, use the spell-check function on your computer to check for spelling and typographical errors. In the second check, carefully

read over the entire document to make sure that nothing was lost or misplaced during the process of embedding the document into the e-mail message.

After you complete this process, click the Send button on your e-mail program and launch your resume.

Putting your resume in an online database

Most commercial recruitment Web sites provide detailed instructions for submitting a resume. In most cases, the instructions are very similar to the procedures for responding to a job posting. The instructions on the Web site may direct you to cut and paste your resume into an online application form or to send your resume to a designated e-mail address.

After you complete the steps for posting a resume at the commercial Web site, wait 48 hours and then search the database to see if you can find your resume.

- If you locate your resume, review it carefully to see if any errors occurred in transmission or processing. If you need to make corrections, follow the procedures that most sites provide for doing so.

- If you cannot locate your resume, contact the site using the e-mail address provided for assistance and questions. In your message, provide your name as it appears on your resume, the date it was sent to the site, and the name of your e-mail service provider. In most cases, Web site managers quickly resolve such situations.

Protecting your privacy

Sending your resume over the Internet to an employer's designated e-mail address is a personal and private communication. The employer is not likely to share that with anyone outside the organization.

Storing your resume in an online resume database, on the other hand, puts that document and the information it contains into the public domain. Your resume is open and available to anyone with access to the database, and in the case of most commercial employment sites, that is any individual or organization paying the access fee — including your current employer.

Although some sites provide a way to block certain organizations from viewing your resume, these systems are not foolproof. After your resume resides in such a database, there is a high probability that other sites may copy it and reproduce in their databases. As a result, there is no fail-safe way to protect the confidentiality of your employment record after you store it online. It is also difficult to prevent an outdated version of your resume from circulating on the Internet forever. You can do two things to protect yourself:

■ Always date your Internet resume so that employers can quickly determine if they are reviewing a current or older version of your employment information.

■ Remove your home address and telephone number from your resume and replace it with an e-mailbox that you use only for employment matters. Check this box frequently, so that you can respond quickly to employer inquiries.

An Internet resume is, without question, an unusual looking document. Despite its appearance, it is a useful document that can help you take advantage of the Internet's resources for finding a new or better job and managing your career.

CLIFFSNOTES REVIEW

Use this CliffsNotes Review to practice what you've learned in this book and to build your confidence in doing the job right the first time. After you work through the review questions, the problem-solving exercises, and the practice projects, you're well on your way to writing a great resume that can help you win the job of your dreams.

Q&A

1. All resumes should include:

    a. Contact information

    b. A description of your workplace experience

    c. Your accomplishments at work

    d. All of the above

2. If your career has progressed steadily through a series of ever more responsible positions, the best resume format for you is

    a. Chronological

    b. Functional

    c. Hybrid

    d. It doesn't really matter

3. A profile

    a. Appears at the end of your resume

    b. Describes the kind of employer for which you want to work

    c. Summarizes your key skills, abilities, experience, and knowledge

    d. Can be omitted if you are a recent college graduate

4. When writing an objective statement, you should be specific and include

    a. The title of the job you're seeking

    b. The kind of place you like to work

    c. The benefit(s) you hope to derive from your employment

    d. All of the above

5. An electronic resume

    a. Is designed for transmission over the Internet

    b. Cannot be reproduced on paper

    c. Does not include underlining or italic

    d. Works best when produced with 10-point type

Answers: (1) d. (2) a. (3) c. (4) d. (5) c.

Scenario

1. Your employer has just announced that the organization is downsizing and that your position will be eliminated.

    You don't have an up-to-date resume and, therefore, can't apply for open positions you see advertised in the newspaper and on the Internet. Your first step is to_____
_____
_____.

2. You decide to use the Internet to search for employment opportunities. You select a Web site where you can view job postings and apply online. Before visiting the site, however, you must make several adjustments to your resume. These include
_____
_____.

3. You left your last position following a dispute with your supervisor. The best way to handle this situation when writing your resume is _____
_____
_____.

Answers: (1) Determine your employment objective. This statement can help you develop a resume with a clear and compelling message about the kind of job you want and your qualifications for such a position. (2) Eliminating all word processing formats, placing selected words in all capital letters for emphasis, shortening the length of text lines, and ending them with a hard return and using plus signs (+) to introduce bullets. (3) To omit it. Potentially negative information is best addressed in an interview, where you should be as straightforward and factual as possible; do not criticize your previous employer or supervisor.

Visual Test

1. Review the following excerpt from the experience section of a resume.

I was responsible for overseeing all sales activities performed by a field team of six agents. Hence, I was accountable for their daily sales performance, lead generation, and account management. My other responsibilities included agent training and development, monthly sales report preparation, key account management, and strategic planning.

What is the primary flaw in this section?

a. It describes the person's tasks in a laundry list with little detail.

b. It uses responsibility statements rather than action verbs to describe what tasks the person performed.

c. It is too short and provides too little information for an employer to evaluate the person's capabilities.

d. There is too much use of the pronoun "I."

Answer: b.

Consider This

Did you know that there are companies that will distribute your resume to hundreds of employers and resume databases on the Internet? You pay a fee for their services, but the expense is usually far less than the cost of sending your resume through the mail. You can choose from several resume distribution companies, including:

- www.employmentzone.com
- www.mailmyresume.com
- www.resumeblaster.com
- www.resumeconnection.com
- www.resumexpress.com

Practice Projects

1. Schedule a performance appraisal with yourself every six months.

2. Use your resume to evaluate your progress in advancing your career. If you have participated in a training program or gained important new experience, update your resume to reflect that additional capability. If, however, you have failed to acquire new skills or experience, your resume will reflect that lack of progress.

3. In either case, set specific goals for the next six months to help you to gain new qualifications that you can then add to your resume.

CLIFFSNOTES RESOURCE CENTER

The learning doesn't need to stop here. CliffsNotes Resource Center shows you the best of the best — links to the best information in print and online about the Internet and its value to your job search and career enhancement. And don't think that this is all — you can find all kinds of pertinent information at www.cliffsnotes.com. Look for all the terrific resources at your favorite bookstore or local library and on the Internet. When you're online, make your first stop www.cliffsnotes.com where you can find more incredibly useful information about finding a job using the Web.

Books

This CliffsNotes title is one of many great books about enhancing your career or finding a new job published by IDG Books Worldwide. So if you want some great next-step books, check out these other publications:

Resumes For Dummies, 2nd Edition, by Joyce Lain Kennedy, is a hands-on guide with over 50 examples for creating resumes that get results. IDG Books, 1999, $12.99.

The Damn Good Resume Guide, by Yana Parker, provides a simple ten-step process for writing a resume that gets results. Ten Speed Press, 1996, $7.95.

Dynamite Resumes, by Ronald L. Krannich, Ph.D. and Caryl Rae Krannich, Ph.D., is a detailed introduction to writing resumes and using them effectively in a job search campaign. Impact Publishing, 1992, $9.95.

Internet Resumes: Take the Net to Your Next Job, by Peter D. Weddle, provides a step-by-step approach to writing a state-of-the-art resume. Impact, 1998, $14.95.

National Business Employment Weekly Resumes, by Taunee Besson, provides a good introduction and numerous illustrations for writing an effective resume. John Wiley & Sons, 1999, $10.95.

The New Perfect Resume, by Tom Jackson and Ellen Jackson, is one of the most popular guides to writing an effective resume. Anchor Press/Doubleday, 1996, $11.95.

Top Secret Resumes & Cover Letters, by Steven Provenzano, is a comprehensive guide to communicating with employers and recruiters. Dearborn Publishing, 1995, $12.95.

100 Winning Resumes for $100,000+ Jobs: Resumes That Can Change Your Life, by Wendy Enelow, describes great senior-level resumes organized by profession. Impact Publications, 1997, $24.95.

You can easily find books published by IDG Books Worldwide, Inc. and other publishers. Check out your favorite bookstores, the library, the Internet, and a store near you. We also have three Web sites that you can use to read about all the books we publish:

■ www.cliffsnotes.com

■ www.dummies.com

■ www.idgbooks.com

Internet

Check out these Web sites for more information about resume-writing:

Damn Good Resumes at www.damngood.com features Yana Parker's resume-writing tips and helpful advice on how to use them.

JobStar California at www.jobsmart.org offers a wide array of information that can help you develop your resume and use it effectively all over the United States.

Career Resumes at www.career-resumes.com is a service operated by Peter Newfield, the "Resume Expert" for the Gonyea Online Career Center on AOL and the "Resume Advisor" for NationJob, a leading commercial employment site on the Internet.

WEDDLE's Publications at www.weddles.com presents an online catalog of books that can help you take full advantage of the resume resources available on the Internet.

Send Us Your Favorite Tips

In your quest for learning, have you ever experienced that sublime moment when you figure out a trick that saves time or trouble? Perhaps you realized you were taking ten steps to accomplish something that could have taken two, or you found a little-known workaround that gets great results. If you've discovered a useful tip that helped you create a winning resume and you'd like to share it, the CliffsNotes staff would love to hear from you. Go to our Web site at www.cliffsnotes.com and click the Talk to Us button. If we select your tip, we may publish it as part of CliffsNotes Daily, our exciting, free e-mail newsletter. To find out more or to subscribe to a newsletter, go to www.cliffs-notes.com on the Web.

INDEX

CliffsNotes™

Your shortcut to
SUCCESS™
for over 40 years

Computers and Software

Confused by computers? Struggling with software? Let *CliffsNotes* get you up to speed on the fundamentals — quickly and easily. Titles include:

Balancing Your Checkbook with Quicken®
Buying Your First PC
Creating a Dynamite PowerPoint® 2000 Presentation
Making Windows® 98 Work for You
Setting up a Windows® 98 Home Network
Upgrading and Repairing Your PC
Using Your First PC
Using Your First iMac™
Writing Your First Computer Program

The Internet

Intrigued by the Internet? Puzzled about life online? Let *CliffsNotes* show you how to get started with e-mail, Web surfing, and more. Titles include:

Buying and Selling on eBay®
Creating Web Pages with HTML
Creating Your First Web Page
Exploring the Internet with Yahoo!®
Finding a Job on the Web
Getting on the Internet
Going Online with AOL®
Shopping Online Safely